THE IRELAND SERIES

PRODUCTION MANAGER
Steve White

EDITORS
Anna Brüning
Colette Dennison

EDITORIAL ASSISTANTS
Gerard Boland
Anna Brüning-White
Steve White

ADVERTISING SALES
Liz McPhillips
Helen Connolly
Rosemary Hand

ART DIRECTORS
Anna Brüning White
Steve White

MAGAZINE DESIGN & LAYOUT
The Graphiconies (Ramaioli)
Pure Drop Productions (White)

COVER DESIGN
Pure Drop Productions (White)

COVER PHOTO
Peter Zöller

COLOUR REPRODUCTION
Nicholson & Bass Ltd.

PRINTING
Nicholson & Bass Ltd.

The Ireland Series is published by
**Euro Lingua Publishing Limited,
12 Parliament Street, Dublin 2.**
Telephone: (01) 679.4291 /
679.1113. Fax: (01) 679.43.86.
This Is Ireland is published annually
by Euro Lingua Publishing Limited.

I reland is one of those countries [...] [...]ng
after you have returned home, long after you have mounted the
photographs, displayed the souvenirs, shelved the guidebooks. In
an unexpected yet evocative way it will come back to visit you.

You may become one of the lucky ones, returning many times to
discover afresh those landscapes which took your breath away, to re-
visit the pub where the musicians played into the early hours and where
the dancers joyously circled and weaved within what seemed an
impossibly confined space. You may look again over the spectacular
Cliffs of Moher and watch the wild Atlantic Ocean crash relentlessly
against the sturdy rocks below. You may even see again some familiar
faces and hear the same old stories Mrs. McGrath told you over breakfast
in her guesthouse, overlooking Galway Bay, those mornings long ago.

Or, you may be content just to remember - the sights, the smells, the
sounds, the encounters, the rain, the wind, the tranquility. Above all, the
tranquility. For many people, Ireland is a tranquil, magical place.

But Ireland is also part of the new Europe. The Irish may be
subconsciously aware of the magical and mystical quality of many
aspects of the country, but most of us are caught up in our daily lives
and do not have time for such luxuries of reflection. Keeping our job,
making sure food is on the table every evening, checking the winning
Lottery numbers - this is the stuff of everyday living for the vast majority
of the population. Ireland may be considered a "First World" country, but
it's a tough struggle to keep one's head above water, to "keep the wolves
from the door". Those who fail to get employment either emigrate or
subsist on or below the official poverty line. That is the harsh reality.

The Ireland Series attempts to describe an Ireland which is multi-
textured, an Ireland of diverse tapestries, an Ireland of many moods.
Within these pages are articles of historical, contemporary, social and
cultural interest. For the visitor there is much you will want, and need, to
know. There are detailed touring itineraries of our spectacular
countryside, comprehensive yet concise Regional directories, and there
is a pictorial gallery of memorable photographs by one of Ireland's
foremost photographers, Liam Blake. The capital city is explored in
detail - in Ann O'Neill's fascinating Walking Tour, and in Seona Mac
Réamoinn's personal eulogy of her home city. Life on some of Ireland's
remote islands is evocatively portrayed by Paul Gosling, and Michael
Viney looks at the unique and fragile coastal and inland ecology of the
mainland.. To help you to decide on what to buy when in Ireland,
Colette Dennison takes you on the shopping trail, and, in another
feature, Liam McAuley journeys through the rich world of Irish music.
A comprehensive examination of modern day Ireland will bring you up
to date with the contemporary situation, while a sensitive portrayal of
Northern Ireland captures the strange mood of hope and desperation
which prevails in this traumatised northern province. And there is more.

Take this journal as your principal guide to Ireland. Regard it as a
collection of selective essays, to dip into when the mood takes you.

However, above all, we hope you enjoy it!

This Is IRELAND

PEOPLE CULTURE LANDSCAPE

ISBN 1 874159 07 6

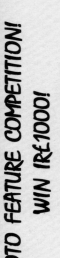

TRAVELOGUE ★

PRACTICAL IRELAND ✕

 Accommodation.   **Places to Shop.**

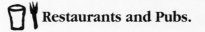**Restaurants and Pubs.**   **Visits and Activities.**

SUBSCRIPTION TO THIS IS IRELAND

If you wish to receive **This Is Ireland** directly to your home address or as a gift to a relative or friend please send your subscription (Eurocheque, postal order or bank draft) along with your address to Euro Lingua Publishing Ltd, Subscriber Services, 12 Parliament Street, Dublin 2, Republic of Ireland

Subscription Rates (inclusive of post & packaging)

	1993 Edition	1994 Edition (Feb. 1994)
UK & Eire	IR £5.95	IR£5.95
USA	US$15.95	US$15.95
CANADA	CAN$15.95	CAN$15.95

The Irish Character

Gerry Boland.

Photo: Peter Zöller

To profess an understanding of the Irish character is to claim a knowledge of the unknowable, a comprehension of the incomprehensible, and a profound weakness for the art of hyperbole. For the Irish character defies categorisation and understanding. In any exploration of our character, a skirting around the edges is all one can ever hope to achieve. To delve deeper is to depart from reality as outsiders know it.

'Provinciality on a grand scale' is how I once heard Ireland and the Irish described. Such a sharp observation, and how nicely put! We may be three-and-a-half million scattered across the land, we may even be a million crammed into the capital city, yet we all know each other. Show me a man from Cork and he'll tell you of his cousins in Donegal and his nieces in Limerick. Show me a woman from Kerry and she'll talk of her sister in Wexford, her uncle in Roscommon, and a battalion of friends and relatives in Dublin. Whenever I am introduced to someone, five minutes has not passed before we discover common friends and, frequently, relatives. It is impossible to be anonymous in Ireland. I have known many people to leave these shores because they could not walk from one end of O'Connell Street to the other without bumping into people they knew. They preferred to take their chance among the anonymous streets of London, Paris, Rome, Dusseldorf or New York.

Walk into any pub on any night of the week in Ireland and you will see the true

BAILEYS®

PLEASURE SHARED...

BAILEYS®

ileys® is a registered trade mark.

Irish extrovert. The male version can be spotted holding court in a noisy circle of encouraging companions. He will be telling tales and slapping backs, drinking a pint and looking occasionally over the shoulders of his companions to see who else he knows, who else is listening, who he can nod to, in casual acknowledgment of their existence. The female version of the species will be sitting in a corner, surrounded by her loyal and trusted confidantes. She will be drinking pints, too, or perhaps a vodka and bitter lemon, a cigarette will be ever present and her distinctive voice and, particularly, her laugh will be audible at a considerable distance. As in every walk of life, exceptions prevail, but the true Irish character is of a sociable

Photo: Peter Zöller

nature. It has been said that a fondness for a 'drop of the hard stuff', or a weakness for the 'pint of plain', explains this extrovertness. Certainly, drink loosens the tongue, facilitates the lowering of built-in self-defence mechanisms, and assists in the important business of exaggeration. And in Ireland exaggeration is an art form.

There was a time when the most common form of exaggeration was found to be in drinking circles. In my early days it was not unusual to hear someone boast that he had drunk sixteen pints of Guinness, driven home, and woken up the following day with no memory whatsoever of his journey home the previous night. Thankfully, a degree of enlightenment has emerged over the past number of years in relation to drinking, driving and exaggerating – nowadays, some still drink and drive, but they no longer boast about it! Most Irish people do not mean to exaggerate, in fact, I am certain most do not even realise they are doing so. Casual exaggeration is more commonly known as white lies. White lies are harmless lies, if any lie can be, in truth, harmless. But, telling our loved ones what they want to hear is not only sensible, it is unquestionably logical.

Disrespect for authority is widespread in Ireland and we have a peculiarly sadistic disrespect for

politicians. Mind you, judging by the way the politicians govern the country, this disrespect is reciprocated in equal measure. I have yet to meet a punter (commonly used term for the ordinary man or woman in the street) who trusts a politician. After all, it is a politician's duty to tell us what we want to hear, and our duty as punters not to believe a word of it. How, then can politicians trust the punter when the same punter keeps voting them out of a job? It is a vicious and suspicious circle.

One often hears about the Irish devotion to religion. Do not believe a word of it. The Irish love to go to mass to see who else is going to mass. We attend funerals with alarming frequency, not because so many people are dying, but because we know so many of them. Our extended circle of friends and relatives can at times be a heavy chain around our necks as we drag ourselves from funeral to funeral. It is true that Catholicism is strong in Ireland and, to a point, the country has been a church-led political state throughout its brief history. But changes are taking place, and this pressure for change has brought out another quality of the Irish character – its fighting spirit.

Those seeking social change draw swords with traditionalists and heated arguments between these two diametrically opposed forces can be heard on a daily basis on our national airwaves. In other spheres, our dogged determination to win against all the odds is amply evidenced by many outstanding, and wholly surprising, wins in the international rugby arena. It would seem that the underdog tag brings out the very best in us. This fighting spirit is best epitomised by the many stories of local communities, under threat of the placement of large multi-national industries on their doorstep, taking up the good fight against powerful industrial and political interests, and winning. This is testimony to the fact that, when browbeaten, we are at our most dangerous. Any foreign government with invasive ideas would be wise to think twice before taking us on!

Belying all this fighting spirit and dogged determination to win against all the odds is the indisputable fact that the Irish are also masters of the laid-back approach. If something can be done tomorrow, why do it today? This approach to life is fine on a small scale but when the whole country is at it, it can be disconcerting, to say the least. A symptom, or perhaps a cause, of this laid-backness is our insatiable appetite for information, Whether it is family, local or national gossip, we all have to know who said what, to whom and why. Our innate curiosity is a perfect excuse to dwell awhile at the garden gate, hover around our colleague's desk, stay a moment longer in the local shop in case we pick up some gossip to bring home. And when we get home we can turn on our radios and listen to the national gossip on the airwaves. Outsiders may call this news, but we Irish know better. It's nothing more than gossip on a grand scale!

Gerry Boland, a native Dubliner, is a freelance writer and tour guide.

Photo: Liam Blake.

Less taxing.

Tax-free.

We don't want you to forget our scenery, or our ability to make you relax. But we also want you to remember that Ireland is a great place for your money if you're a non-resident. And Bank of Ireland can offer you:

• Complete security and confidentiality.

• The flexibility of withdrawal on demand - but an even higher rate of interest if you deposit your money with us for more than thirty days.

• The convenience of depositing your money in Irish pounds or any other major currency, by post or via any bank worldwide.

If you'd like to send your money to Ireland to grow, fill in the coupon and we'll send you more information on tax-free savings with Bank of Ireland.

Nous ne voulons pas vous laisser oublier notre paysage ou les possibilités que nous vous donnons de vous détendre. Nous voulons cependant vous rappeler que l'Irlande est le lieu idéal de placement de votre argent si vous êtes non-résident. La Bank of Ireland vous offre:

• Une sécurité et une confidentialité absolues.

• Facilités de retraits à vue et un taux d'intérêt encore plus élevé si vous nous laissez votre argent en dépôt pendant plus de trente jours.

• La possibilité de déposer votre argent en livres irlandaises ou toute autre monnaie par la poste ou par l'intermédiaire de n'importe quelle banque mondiale.

Si vous désirez envoyez votre argent en Irlande pour le faire fructifier, remplissez le coupon ci-joint et nous vous enverrons des renseignements complémentaires concernant une épargne exempte d'impôts avec la Bank of Ireland.

Irland ist bekannt für seine landschaftlichen Reize und für seinen Erholungswert. Wußten sie jedoch, daß auch Irh Geld in Irland gut aufgehoben ist, wenn Sie Devisenausländer sind. Bank of Ireland bietet Ihnen:

• Absolute Sicherheit und Diskretion.

• Flexibilität - ihr Geld ist jederzeit behebbar, mit noch besseren Zinssätzen bei Bindung für mindestens 30 Tage.

• Eine bequeme Möglichkeit, Ihr Geld in irischen Pfund oder einer anderen größeren Währung per Post oder über jede beliebige Bank in aller Welt einzuzahlen.

Wenn Sie Ihr Geld in Irland anlegen möchten, um gute Erträge zu ernten, füllen Sie einfach den Coupon aus und Sie erhalten von uns umgehend Informationen über steuerfreies Sparen mit der Bank of Ireland.

Non vogliamo che dimenticate i ns. paessaggi o la ns. capacità de farVi rilassare. Ma se siete 'Non-residenti', vogliamo anche ricordarVi che è opportuno investire il Vostro denaro in Irlanda. La Bank of Ireland Vi offre:

• Completa sicurezza e riservatezza.

• La possibilità de prelevare a richiesta. Inoltre, se il denaro rimane depositato presso le nostre casse per più de 30 giorni consecutivi, matura un tasso d'interesse maggiore.

• La scelta di versare il denaro in Lire irlandesi oppure in qualsiasi delle altre valute principali. Il versamento può essere effettuato a mezzo posta o tramite banca, nazionale o all'estero.

Se desiderate investire il Vostro denaro in Irlanda, inviateci il modulo seguente, debitamente compilato. Noi Vi trasmetteremo tutte le informazioni sulle agevolazioni fiscali disponibili con la Bank of Ireland.

NON-RESIDENT ACCOUNT

Name/Nom/Name/Nome

_____

Address/Adresse/Anschrift/Indirizzo

_____

_____

_____

Tel: _____

Please send me further information about a Bank of Ireland Non-Resident Account.

Veuillez m'adresser des renseignements complémentaires sur les comptes de non-résidents de Bank of Ireland.

Bitte senden Sie mir weitere Informationen über die Einrichtung eines Ausländerkontos bei der Bank of Ireland.

Vi prego di inviarmi ulteriori informazioni riguardante i Conti di Risparmio per Non-residenti presso la Bank of Ireland.

Please tick whether the account would be in IR£
Cocher si ce compte est en IR£
Bitte kreuzen Sie an, ob das Konto in IR£
Indicare P.F. se il conto sarà in IR£

Any other major currency
Toute autre monnaie majeure
Einer anderen größeren Währung geführt werden soll
Altra valuta principale

Send coupon to/ Veuillez adresser le coupon à l'adresse suivante/Diesen Abschnitt bitte einsenden an/inviate il modulo a:
New Business Manager - DM, Bank of Ireland PO Box 2103, Dublin 2, Ireland.

Bank of Ireland

Helping to make things happen.

IS /93   **INFORMATION HOTLINE DUBLIN 295 9000**

▼ HISTORICAL ▼ RESUME

BC

Approx. 8000BC.	First inhabitants of Ireland.
Approx. 4000-3000 BC.	Arrival of New Stoneage Man and megalithic culture.
Approx. 200 BC.	Arrival of the Gaels.

AD

431-432 AD	St. Patrick arrives and christianises Gaels.
7th and 8th centurys	Christian Golden Age (illuminated manuscripts)
791	Vikings land in the south.
988	Major wave of Vikings arrive in Dublin.
1014	High King, Brian Boru, defeats Vikings at Clontarf.
1169-1170	Norman invasion who within 100 years rule 3/4's of the country.
13thC,14thC &15thC	Wars and counter attacks.
1534	Introduction of Reformation causes religious conflict.
1601	English defeat Irish chieftains and Spanish at Kinsale.
1605	English law enforced throughout Ireland.
1628	Confiscated lands settled with "planters" from England and Scotland.
1641	Rebellion over lands.
1649-50	Cromwell, enforcing Reformation, devasted Ireland.
1690	Accession dispute in England leads to the Battle of the Boyne between Catholic James II and Protestant William of Orange, who wins.
1695	Penal Laws against Catholics.
1782	Strivings for freedom results in Independent Parliament in Dublin.

1796-1798	Various armed struggles for freedom (incl. Wolfe Tone with French fleet at Bantry Bay).
1800	"Act of Union", Ireland again under direct rule from Westminster.
1829	Parliamentarian, Daniel O'Connell achieves Catholic Emancipation.
1845 - 49	Series of famines devastate Ireland.
1858	Founding of various freedom organisations (Fenians etc.)
1879 - 82	Land War.
1895	Gaelic movements gain momentum.
1905 - 1912	Land Purchases Acts, Irish Home Rule Bill; English tardiness provokes Irish volunteer armies.
1916	Easter rising defeated by English troops. De Valera elected MP.
1919 - 21	War of Independence.
1921 - 22	Civil war. Establishment of Free State (6 Northern counties opt for UK union).
1927	De Valera's Fianna Fail party elected.
1937	Constitution of "Eire". New economic and military agreements with UK.
1949	"Republic of Ireland" declared (UK guarantees support for Northern Ireland).
1969	Unrest in Northern Ireland leads to the dispatch of British troops and province placed under direct rule.
1973	Ireland joins EEC.
1988	Dublin celebrates it's millenium as a city.
1991	Dublin - "European City of Culture".

When the locals want something special they come to

BLARNEY

Woollen Mills

Blarney, Co. Cork.

The Great Irish Shopping Experience.

The best selection of traditional and classic sweaters anywhere in Ireland. The best quality and at the right price. The finest of Irish gifts. The famous Irish welcome and friendly atmosphere. The great Irish shopping experience.

Blarney, Co.Cork. Tel: (021) 385280 and Nassau St., Dublin. Tel: (01) 710068

Ireland

THROUGH THE LENS OF
LIAM BLAKE

4

5

7

8

9

10

11

15

16

17

20

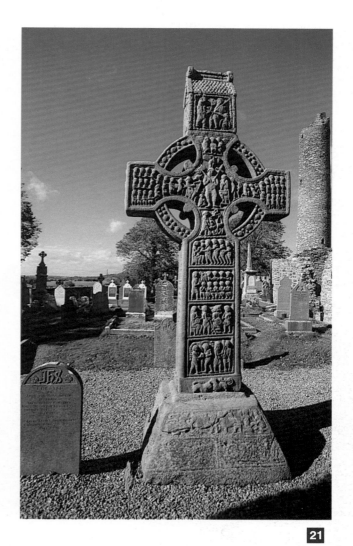

21

22

24

25

26

27

28

31

32

34

Liam Blake, a Dubliner, developed.an early curiosity and interest in photography. Following on from his work as a lithographic printer he became a professional photographer.

He has gained a wide reputation for his photographs of people and landacapes for the "Real Ireland" series of postcards which set new trends in this area.

Liam has won several prestigious awards in particular the "Kilkenny Book Design Award". Books illustrated with his photographs include among others, "Real Ireland 1984" and "Portraits of Ireland 1985".

Three renowned Dublin galleries, the Douglas Hyde Gallery, the Riverrun Gallery and the Gallery of Photography have exhibited his works.

Liam Blake lives in south Dublin.

Photographic Feature - Captions.

1. Standing Stone, Clogher, Dingle Penninsula.
2. Mulligans Pub, Dublin.
3. Trinity College Dublin.
4. Killarney & Reeks.
5. Dingle Penninsula, Co. Kerry.
6. Couple & Cottage, Mallow, Co. Cork.
7. Pilgrims, Croagh Patrick, Co. Mayo.
8. Pub, Allihies, West Cork.
9. Itinerants, Bride Street, Dublin.
10. Sunset, Sky Road, Clifden, Connemara.
11. Currach Race, Carraroe, Connemara.
12. Twelve Bens, Connemara.
13. Turf Stack & Twelve Bens, Connemara.
14. Connemara Golf Club.
15. Beara Penninsula, West Cork.
16. Beara Penninsula, West Cork.
17. Beach & Blaskets, Slea Head, Dingle.
18. Ballinakill Harbour, Co. Galway.
19. Skelligs & Puffin Island, Ring of Kerry.
20. Round Tower, Glendalough, Co. Wicklow.
21. Monasterboice High Cross, Co. Louth.
22. Staigue Fort, Sneem, Ring of Kerry.
23. Sunset Over Liffey, Dublin City Centre.
24. Cottage at Dusk, Connemara.
25. Dunguaire Castle, Kinvara, Co. Galway.
26. Pilgrims, Croagh Patrick, Co. Mayo.
27. "Local" in Clifden, Co. Galway.
28. "At the Races"- Dingle, Co. Kerry.
29. Ennistymon, Co. Clare.
30. Shop Front, Skibbereen, Co. Cork.
31. Tree, Maam Valley, Connemara, Co. Galway.
32. Bog Cutting, Co. Galway.
33. Cottage under Mt. Brandon, Dingle Penninsula.
34. Pub and Undertaker, Navan, Co. Meath.
35. Westport, Co. Mayo.

35

Trinity College
Walking Tours

In 1992 Trinity College celebrates the 400th anniversary of it's foundation. You can enjoy a guided walking tour of the college in the company of one of Trinity Tours experienced and officially approved guides taking in the magnificent **Book of Kells** and the new **Collonades Gallery** in the Old Library.

Dublin
Footsteps

- a series of daily walking tours from May to September.

(A) Walk Back 1000 Years
(B) Literary Footsteps
(C) 18th Century Dublin
(D) The Evening Tour

Tours A, B, C & D operate 3 times daily from Bewley's Museum on Grafton Street.

All tours are conducted by experienced Dublin City guides. Information on all tours can be obtained from Tourist Information Offices, hotels and guesthouses in Dublin.

Tel: 01/6794291   Fax: 01/6794386

Spoil Yourself!

Enjoy the glamorous life of Adare Manor...from afternoon teas in the Drawing Room to candlelit dinners in the Dining Room or Gallery, to fireside drinks in the Library or Tack Room.

Home for the past two centuries to the Earls of Dunraven, Adare manor has been lovingly transformed into a world-class hotel with sixty-four luxury bedrooms. Located only 20 miles from Shannon Airport in Ireland's most picturesque village of Adare. The Manor's 840 acre estate offers horse riding, walks, fishing, golf.

Adare Festival July 9th - 26th.
The best of contemporary and classical music in a spectacular setting.

Tel: 061-396566. Telex: 70733. Fax: 061-396124.
USA toll-free reservations: 1-800-462-3273 (Go Adare)

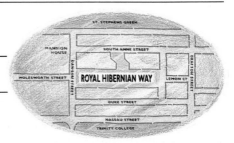

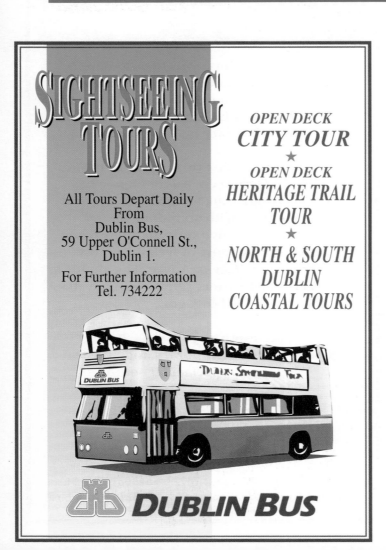
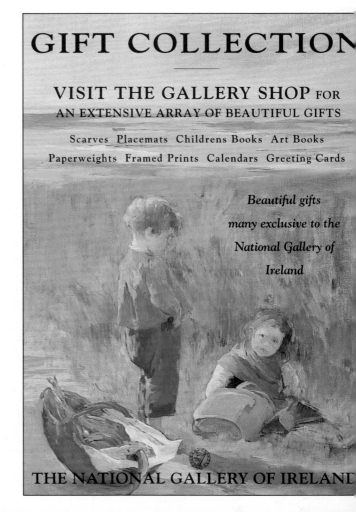

Photo: Peter Zöller

Seona Mac Réamoinn

Dublin is undoubtedly a capital city, the centre of government, commerce and culture in Ireland. It is unnervingly racially homogeneous but surprisingly culturally cosmopolitan. In the tradition of all interesting cities it is also somewhat unpredictable and full of contradictions. Dubliners are both innately curious and respectful of privacy. They are more interested in the detail of life in Milan than in Mullingar, but Hollywood stars and distinguished writers, infamous rock musicians can move easily through the city, recognised but not harassed. The city is small in size and therefore seems quickly familiar, yet it retains an ability to startle and to allow for individual discoveries. These can be people or places or as often in Ireland, both intertwined. It is the city of Joyce's Ulysses, but reading the novel is not enough. As Leopold Bloom discovered, the best way to begin to understand any city is to take to the streets, seek vantage points for observing but first find a perspective. In Dublin, this is the river.

The river Liffey, the Anna Livia of James Joyce, flows eastwards through the centre of the city and acts as a physical if not at times a psychological divide. Even today, northsiders and southsiders continue a tradition of humorous competitiveness on the merits and flaws of either side. However, the city actually began on the south bank of the river and geographically the oldest part of the city is located a little west of O'Connell Bridge and the city centre. A Viking settlement, its name in Irish is Baile Atha Cliath, "the city of the ford of the hurdles" and in these times it became a thriving town of trade and commerce. Indeed in the reign of the first city father, Sitric Silkenbeard, the first coinage of the city was minted. Street names in the area bear witness to this with Winetavern Street, High Street and Exchange Street. A Towering Inferno of Concrete housing the civic offices somewhat mars the view of history, but no doubt visitors to the city can produce their own versions of witless city planning! The Vikings clearly exposed the strategic potential of the city and thereafter we hosted a series of not always welcome guests, including the Normans and our neighbours from Britain. Most of the influences of these temporary rulers have seeped into the character and style of Dublin but others are still visible, notably some fine architectural bequests. The Bank of Ireland on College Green, Trinity College, Dublin Castle – all places

Relaxing in Saint Stephen's Green. Photo: Peter Zöller.

which are also worthy of comment. As well as a mosque and a synagogue the city has two twelfth century cathedrals, Christ Church and St. Patricks, both belonging to the Protestant Church of Ireland and located within a half mile of each other in the heart of medieval Dublin. St. Patricks is not just associated with religion but with literature, for the Dean of the Cathedral from 1713 to 1745 was Jonathan Swift, writer, commentator and satirical polemicist and the cathedral abounds in memorials of his life. The surprising point is that the dominant Catholic Church can only boast a modest Pro-Cathedral, (sited off O'Connell.Street) a mere stand-in for a fully fledged edifice. The local dry observation on this anomaly is "Two amateurs, one pro"! Incidentally, professional ghouls might be attracted by the conserved corpses in the old crypts of St. Michans, an 11th century church which lies directly north across the river from Christ Church.

For the next specific vantage point you should take yourself back to the city centre or An Lár (Irish for "the centre"), the terminus of many bus routes. O'Connell Bridge and O'Connell Street, in many ways represent a perfect vignette of the contrasts and contradictions of Dublin. A broad boulevard, competing as the widest street in Europe, it is a haven of fast food and neon, conspiring to be bustling and cosmopolitan with just a hint of danger and revealing some of the more uncomfortable aspects of large urban centres. In the outer suburbs of Darndale, Neilstown and parts of Tallaght, the deprivation resulting from high concentrations of unemployment is particularly evident, although far removed from the usual tourist trail. But even as you cross O'Connell Bridge and start to walk up O'Connell Street, you will meet children begging, a highly visible sign of the underside of prosperous city life in most societies.

As you continue up the street, it is a curious paradise for the customer. Bunches of flowers, cheap jewelry, silk scarves or a copy of Frankfurter Allgemeine are all on sale from street vendors. Then you will reach the columns of the GPO (The General Post Office) and initiation is beginning. In 1916 a military rising began within the walls of the GPO and a proclamation of the aims was read by Patrick Pearse, one of the leaders. They are inscribed on a statue of Cuchulainn, the mythic Ulster hero, which still stands among the signs for Stamps and Poste Restante. Outside, you are likely to encounter the dark form of the fervently eccentric Catholic woman, complete with crucifix who daily incants her own personal religious ritual and then side by side, a rally seeking liberalisation of the laws on divorce and contraception. Ironically enough, all of this within a few hundred yards of the Rotunda Hospital

where power and wisdom were dispersed – are such exhibits, but particularly the magnificence of the Georgian architect James Gandon. Gandon designed three major public buildings for the city and while a brief rampage of planning and neglect allowed large sections of 18th and 19th century Dublin to vanish into the rubbled mist of time, there has been recent refurbishment and renovation of public buildings. Gandon's restored Custom House now looms in illuminated splendour over the river, a harbinger of vitality returning to the city.

Before setting out to choose some further vantage points and to explore some of the contradictions of the city, river lore briefly intervenes, as the Liffey offers a vital clue to finding your way around. There is no grid pattern to follow and street signs often compound the problem by changing their names every 300 yards. Unusually, a street has a "bottom" and a "top" end. Locals will give you directions which may begin "Go to the top of Grafton St." Do not be confused. This is, of course, the end which is farthest away from the river, close to St. Stephen's Green, while the "bottom" always slopes to the bank of the river and is located around Trinity College. There is also the question of "upper" and "lower" in some city streets but perhaps this should be part of your own discovery plan ... As we begin to walk around the city, a sense of history, literature and place, all are absorbed into streets and buildings, separately, or all at once. At times, it will be difficult to extract any linear structure of its history but there are always curious observations to be made and contradictions can first emerge in places of political or religious importance or intrigue. For instance, the site of the original Irish Parliament (dating from 1792) now belongs to the commercial Bank of Ireland. But, the House of Lords is wonderfully restored and is open to the public during banking hours, while coal fires warm the chilly corridors of commerce during the winter months. We can move from politics to religion, or in this case, from Mammon to God and find places of worship

Dublin by the Sea.
Sailing on Dublin Bay.
Photo: Eamonn Farrell.

dating from 1752 and the first purpose – built maternity hospital in Europe. The hospital also houses the Gate Theatre within its walls, a rival to the National Abbey Theatre in performing the work of national and international playwrights.

Dublin's Rich Georgian Heritage. Bord Failte Photo.

It is important to enjoy these ironies. Dubliners revel in them. It helps deflect attention from explaining the unexplainable and taking the serious to the level of the sublime. A modern fountain sculpture with a figure of Anna Livia invoking the river as a lifeline of the city was recently installed in O'Connell Street. City wits competed to give it a comic contemporary name and "the floosie in the jacuzzi" was declared the winner. And so it is too with important historical events like that revolution which began in a post office or, as a character in a play by contemporary playwright Frank Mc Guinness pithily described poet and patriot Patrick Pearse: ..."the boy who took over a post office because he was short of a few stamps."

Moving south of the river you will come to our next chosen observation deck, Trinity College. This oasis, masquerading as a landmark is currently celebrating 400 years as a university. The gates, while guarded by statues of two of its famous graduates, poet and dramatist, Oliver Goldsmith, and philosopher and statesman Edmund Burke, are open to everyone. The eighth century illuminated manuscripts of the Book of Kells are on view in the Library but don't forget to wander around imposing Front Square or in the summer watch a game of cricket while the leisurely order of academic and student life is undisturbed by the noise and hassle of the capital city in motion outside the walls.

A short walk further and you are now at Bewleys Cafe on Grafton Street. If you can find a seat on the mezzanine level you can have a perfect view of Grafton Street, the premier shopping street of the city but where street life endeavours to distract and delay the passers by as they move from Trinity College to St. Stephen's Green. You can watch colourful flower sellers, mime artists, or fire eaters and listen to an extraordinary medley of musical styles as free-form jazz is suddenly drowned by frenzied fiddle players. But Bewleys is actually the point of observation. Here is where you begin to concentrate on the people of the city, stalking them to the places where they gather together.

Bewleys Oriental Cafes, founded by a Quaker family, are now owned by a corporation and they are the closest

you will get to Dublin cafe society. Although now offering franchised operations and surfacing quite inappropriately in Cork, Galway and Belfast, they are best savoured in their original locations; on Westmoreland Street and Grafton Street. They offer dark wood and marbled tables, sticky buns, steaming coffee and stunning stained glass windows by Harry Clarke, Ireland's foremost stained glass artist. Their patrons include priests, politicians and punks and while poetry readings, lunchtime plays, and cappuccinos till 2 am are recent additions, they remain a Dublin institution to be missed at your peril.

The other institution is Arthur Guinness, whose brewery is still sited in the city and has a Visitors Centre where you can have a free sample of the brew. It is best however, tasted in its natural habitat, a Dublin pub. An invitation to "go for a pint" is a blithe understatement of the activity that takes place in a Dublin pub. In the plush mirrored bar of the Shelbourne or the dark panelled snug of Ryans of Parkgate Street, people gather to exchange news, gossip, scandal, to trade fact with fantasy, to discuss anything from Schopenhauer to sport with equal attention and, incidentally, to drink. Although pubs in Dublin offer live music sessions ranging from traditional to jazz, blues and especially rock, they are primarily noted for the rattle and hum of conversation. Novelist Flann O'Brien (1911-1966) who also wrote newspaper columns under the pen name "Myles na gCopaleen", humorously asserting the authority of Dublin in matters of language and whiskey wrote:

"The best English is spoken in Dublin.
The best Irish is drunk in Dublin.
The best Irish are drunk in Dublin!"

Typical Dublin Pub. Photo: Eamonn Farrell

Visitors to the city are constantly amazed by the style of pubgoing. Why should even government ministers eschew the quiet comfort of an empty bar and prefer to stand for hours crushed in the overcrowded corner of a smoke filled pub next door, elbowing their way to the bar, just to have a pint of Guinness? No answer. However, there are idyllic moments to be stolen in quiet Dublin pubs in the afternoons. When the scent of malt from the Guinness Brewery hangs high in the air, it is time to withdraw to a dark shadowed pub with the sunlight filtering gently through the door and have idle conversation with the bartender, or perhaps not talk at all...

Much talk but no action characterised attempts to improve the scape and shape of the city but now, being idle for too long, the city has begun to actively take pride in itself and is attempting to match the sprawl of urban decay with a surge of urban renewal. There are now tax incentives to attract business and residential development and to lure people back into the city. North of the river the potential success is the Financial Services Centre, a complex of international banking institutions, with planning also for appartments and restaurants. Temple Bar, lying between Dame Street and the south quays of the Liffey is another, more vibrant example of renewal in action. It is also a good place to observe a different aspect of the city, an indicator of change and of a cultural energy that has placed Dublin in the forefront of international cities for music, theatre, art and film, quite disproportionately, as always, to its size! The tradition and international reputation of Bram Stoker, Sean O'Casey,

Top: Night Life, Temple Bar. Photo: Timothy Kovar.
Middle: Street Traders, Moore Street. Bord Failte Photo.
Bottom: Street Musicians, Grafton Street. Photo: Eamonn

art and sport which take place at various times throughout the year.

With all that talk of art, one is inclined to forget about the great sporting culture of the city and a perfect opportunity to observe the denizens of the city is to follow them as they watch their favourite game. Team sports are very popular and in almost all areas of the city and suburbs there are weekend games with strong and loyal local support. While the Dublin Horse Show and international rugby or soccer matches all have a good atmosphere, there is nothing quite like an afternoon at Croke Park for a championship game of Gaelic football or hurling and it is yet another occasion to make a few cultural observations. There is a wonderful cross section of Irish society present and a game at Croke Park attracts men, women and children, from all walks of life. It is also about the only time when Dubliners are reasonably tolerant about the city being invaded as battalions of supporters converge on the capital from other parts of the country. The prominent seats at the match are usually occupied by leading members of the government and the clergy, happily exhibiting common ground in Church/State relationships and the general

Joyce, Beckett, Kavanagh has been passed on to another generation of artists in the city. Some are writers but others are film makers or musicians and rock band U2 and the Oscar winning film, My Left Foot, belong very much to the city of Dublin. Temple Bar itself is a pedestrianised maze of small narrow streets full of galleries and recording studios, cafes and artists studios, antique clothing stores and restaurants. Saved from being transformed into a major bus depot, Temple Bar is now a designated conservation area with hotels and apartments also planned. While compared (somewhat fancifully) to the Left Bank of Paris there are moments on summer nights when there is a marked continental feel as myriad young people take to meeting and drinking on the cobbled streets. The Irish Film Centre, located in a renovated Quaker Meeting House, and the nearby Project Arts Centre are among those offering an alternative menu of cinema and theatre to that available in the mainstream cultural palaces. And all of this without mentioning the wide range of carnivals and special festivals in the city encompassing music, theatre, film,

partisan atmosphere, heightened if the "Dubs" are playing!

Too soon, a visit to Dublin will be over and like the supporters from Kerry or Donegal after a match in the capital, you will have to return home. If you have approached the city correctly, and allowed yourself to be distracted in pubs, in bookshops and in conversations there will be so much left undone, thereby creating a perfect reason to come back The unvisited art galleries and museums, the unexplored streets and squares, the inexplicable humour and accent of the people you met will all have to be put aside for further investigation. You may have time to travel out of the city in the steps of Ulysses as far as Howth or Sandycove, but currently there is an exuberance of mood and a spirit of confidence filling the city which could successfully conspire to keep you engaged within its millennium walls.

Seona Mac Réamoinn is a freelance journalist. A native Dubliner, she lives and works in the city centre.

D U B L I N
ON FOOT

Ann O'Neill

Let's go for a walk around town! "Around" in the true sense of the word. We can either join one of the organised walking tours (details from Beatrice"s Guiding Service, Tel: 545943), or else follow the programme specially drawn up here. Either is fine but it's more fun to join a walking party with different nationalities and to have, at your disposal, a real Dublin guide from whom you can ask any question you like.

1).Bewley's Cafe, our meeting point, is one of the three cafes founded in Dublin by the Bewley family. Their company has specialised in importing tea and coffee since 1840. The Grafton Street cafe was built on the site of an old school which had some illustrious names among its pupils, names like the Duke of Wellington (who beat Napoleon at Waterloo), Richard Brinsley Sheridan, the dramatist, and Thomas Moore, poet and friend of Lord Byron. Later James Joyce, Patrick Kavanagh and practically all the poets and writers in Dublin came to Bewley's to observe and be observed while they sipped the wonderful Bewley's coffee.

2).Grafton Street is a pedestrian street equally attractive to visitors and to Dubliners. There's always a carnival atmosphere with singers, musicians, jugglers and clowns putting on their shows against a background of splendid nineteenth century buildings. At the end of Grafton Street is Duke Street which has two pubs mentioned by James Joyce in 'Ulysses' : The Bailey conserves the actual door of the house (7 Eccles Street) where Joyce's

fictional representation, Leopold Bloom, lived, while Davy Byrne's is the pub where Joyce dined on that memorable day.

Further on along Grafton Street is Harry Street which has McDaid's, the famous literary pub of the 40's and 50's. The poets Patrick Kavanagh, Flann O'Brien and Brendan Behan were habitués of this pub and sometimes were to be

found in a small room at the back known as the 'reanimation room'. Every now and then Brendan Behan would be barred for being too drunk. Being barred was a tough punishment for a

drinker. A certain fellow used to boast that he would have to take a taxi and go five miles out of the city before finding a pub he wasn't barred from. We've talked a good bit about pubs but it shouldn't be thought that you have to drink alcohol in them. All pubs also serve non-alcoholic drinks, coffee and good quality food. Before leaving Grafton Street, don't miss Powerscourt Townhouse, just a stone's throw behind Bewley's Cafe. This refurbished eighteenth-century great house has a covered internal courtyard with restaurants, shops, antique and craft emporia.

3). On **St Stephen's Green** there's a wonderful park with a small artificial lake, so well-known that it is impossible to grow up in Dublin without feeding the ducks on the lake. It was Lord Ardilaun, the Guinness producer, who in the 19th century dreamed up this park with its flower-beds, lake for aquatic wild life, bandstand and deck chairs for taking the sun. There's a beautiful sculpture by Henry Moore commemorating the poet W B Yeats and on the southern side a simple bust of James Joyce looking towards number 86 St Stephen's Green, a part of The National University, where Joyce studied at the end of the last century. Number 86 has decorative plasterwork on its walls and ceilings while the courteous caretaker will show you a photograph of Joyce at the entrance. On the west side of the square the building with the columns is the Royal College of Surgeons which was held by the rebels for a brief period during the Easter Rising of 1916. Just beside it is the St Stephen's Green Centre, a modern shopping centre with luminous and lively arcades, cafes and one of the largest chain stores in Ireland.

4).Dawson Street. The most conspicuous building on Dawson Street is the Mansion House, residence of the Lord Mayor of Dublin. Built at the beginning of the 18th century, it has the arms of the city of Dublin on its pediment. Just beside it is the Royal Irish Academy founded in the 18th century to keep the old Irish treasures which were later transferred to the national Museum. The windows on the side of the Academy were walled up because some members of staff had the habit of standing behind them and making faces at the Lord Mayor. On the other side of the Academy is St Anne's, an 18th century church with an elaborate facade but a very simple interior. Further on, on the other side, is the Hibernian Way, a narrow street joining Dawson and Grafton Streets and which boasts some elegant shops and a rôtisserie, an excellent spot for eating and drinking.

5). Kildare Street. At the Stephen's Green end of Kildare Street stands the Shelbourne Hotel, a large distinguished hotel built almost 200 years ago. It has an "olde worlde" reception room where afternoon tea can be taken in luxury. There is also a sophisticated cocktail bar, "The Horsehoe Bar", which is always crowded but packed to the gills during Horse Show Week (early August). Further along Kildare Street is the National Museum, with its unique exhibitions of gold and silver Celtic art, early Christian chalices and varied pottery. Opposite the museum there's a house with a plaque in memory of Bram Stoker, who lived there and who wrote about and invented Dracula. Beyond the Museum is Leinster House, a Georgian building, presently the seat of the Irish government, where one can on occasion have a guided tour provided one has identification papers (passport or identity card). On the other side is the double of the Museum, the National Library, where the rarest and most precious Irish manuscripts are kept. At the end of the street, looking onto Trinity College is a magnificent building, nowadays the Alliance Française but in the past the Kildare Street Club, a gambling club for rich 19th century officials and landowners which was decorated by a mischievous mason with monkeys and other animals playing billiards.

Illustrations: Donal Teskey

6). Merrion Square is a marvellous public park surrounded by imposing Georgian houses with characteristic large windows and pannelled doors. On the west side of the square, on either side of Leinster House, are the Natural History Museum and the national Art Gallery, the latter with a good collection of works by Irish as well as Italian, Flemish and English painters. On the right, in front of the Gallery, is a small statue of George Bernard Shaw, the author of St Joan,

Pygmalion etc. Shaw in his will left an enormous sum of money to the Gallery in thanks for the happy hours spent there during his solitary adolescence. Another adolescence was spent in no 1 Merrion Square - that of Oscar Wilde, ingenious and witty Dubliner.

7). Trinity College - an oasis of peace in the heart of the city which this year celebrates its 400 year anniversary. The university was founded in 1592 and was the alma mater of Oscar Wilde, Jonathan Swift and Samuel Beckett. It has seven libraries with eight and a half million books. The Book of Kells, an illuminated manuscript of the Gospels written in the 8th century, can be seen in the Old Library, a library which is rich in atmosphere. On no account should this exquisitely written and illustrated book be missed. Also highly recommended is a guided walking tour of Trinity College and a visit to the Dublin Experience and the Colonades. All of these can be arranged through Trinity Tours (Tel: 01-6794291) or directly at Trinity College (Tel: 01 772941).

8). College Green. During the Middle Ages, College Green was a large sports field; now the Bank of Ireland occupies it. This building was constructed in 1729 as home of the Irish Parliament and is as grandiose today as when it was built. It is possible, during banking hours (10.00 - 15.00), to see the magnificent, restored House of Lords.

9). Dame Street. Off Dame Street one can find Dublin Castle, which was built in 1204 but restored during the Georgian period. Formerly the symbol of English power in Ireland the Castle now contains the State Apartments which are open to the public. Here one can admire Irish furniture and carpets and the dazzling crystal of Waterford. The nearby CIty Hall (1767) is the town hall wherein the Lord Mayor and his administration meet every week.

10). Christchurch Cathedral was built in 1172 and has splendid vaulted crypts whose walls are steeped in history. During the Middle Ages these crypts were used as markets and even as taverns. They were so turbulent that Trinity College students were not allowed to go there. We are now in the heart of Old Dublin, where the Vikings founded the city in the 9th century. Nearby are the Liberties, a popular quarter going back to the 12th century.

The Guinness Brewery is not too far from here (only a ten minute walk from Christchurch). On Fishamble Street, in a theatre which unfortunately doesn't exist anymore, Handel's "Messiah", sung by the choirs of the cathedrals of Christchurch and St Patrick's, had its first performance in 1742. You can find a commemorative plaque on the wall of Kennan's Steelworks.

11). St Patrick's is another medieval cathedral a stone's throw from Christchurch and is the last stop on our tour. This is the oldest Christian site in the city. This is where St Patrick built a church in the 5th century. The present church was built in 1190 and restored during the 19th century. It is now the national cathedral for Irish Protestants. If you can manage to visit during

Matins (10.45) or during Vespers (17.45) you will be privileged to hear some beautiful music. There has been a choir school in St Patrick's since 1432. Jonathan Swift, the great writer and

humourist, was dean of this church from 1713 to 1745 and will always be remembered in Dublin for his generosity to the poor and also for his love for (at least) two women - Stella and Vanessa.

Behind St Patrick's there is a park with a literary walk carrying the names of twelve Irish writers on plaques mounted in a wall. Nearby is the Iveagh Trust, a block of Victorian flats in red brick, built in 1900 to replace old ruined houses. After this long walk it's time to go back to Grafton Street (passing by Stephen's Street and Chatham Street) and to Bewley's for a well-deserved cup of coffee and "traditional sticky buns".

39

Anne O'Neill is a qualified Dublin city guide who has been organising walking tours of Dublin for the past four years.

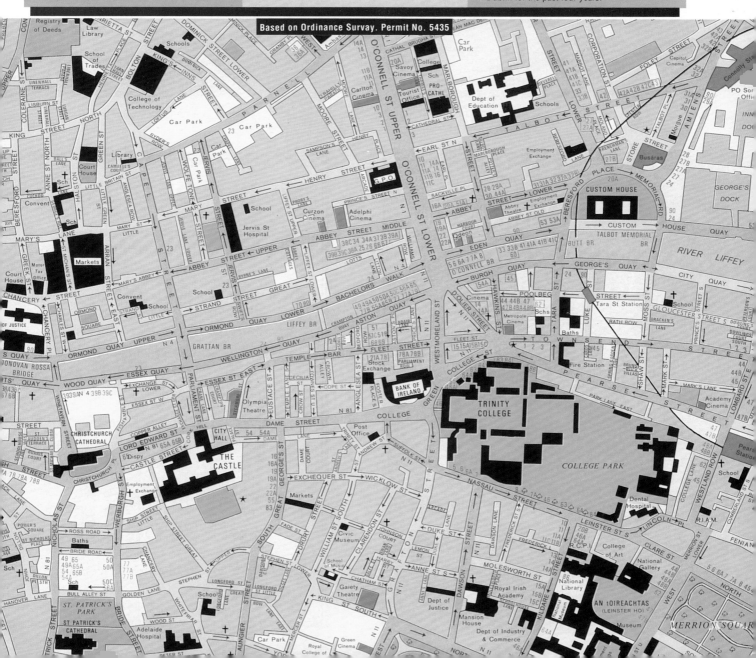

Based on Ordinance Survey. Permit No. 5435

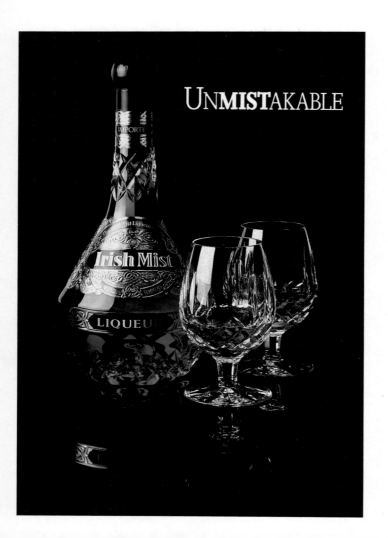

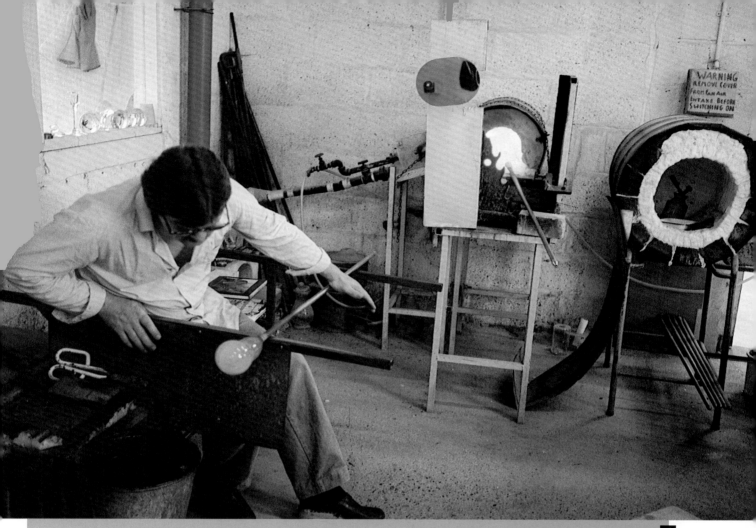

Quality made in Ireland

Colette Dennison.

It might seem paradoxical that so small a country as Ireland can boast the largest craft industry in Europe, if not in the world, but it is in fact the home of not just exquisite Waterford glass and chunky Aran sweaters but also of the world's finest tweeds, linen, woollens and lace.

Whether you are looking for classic clothing in natural fibres, soft furnishings in wool and mohair, sweaters or shawls, pottery or perfume, linen or lace, jackets or jewellery, Ireland is a rare Aladdin's cave for the traveller who appreciates quality fused with tradition.

Indeed when one looks into Irish shop windows, be they clinging to the side of a mountain or on a trendy Dublin street, tradition is very much to the fore with the marriage of modern sophisticated styles and high fashion consciousness to customary fabrics and materials.

Mention the word 'Waterford' wherever you are in the world and the response will undoubtedly be 'glass', say the word 'Aran' and the first thing that springs to mind is 'sweater'. These are just two of the innumerable top quality hand-crafted goods made with the fines of Irish materials that have found their way onto the international market far away from the windswept shores of this island.

We Irish are so used to our tweeds and woollens, our linen and lace, not to mention our smoked salmon and smooth Irish whiskeys that all too often we forget what attractive purchases they can be for our foreign visitors.

Our hand woven tweeds for instance, which can be bought by the metre, echo the heather purple mountains, russet bogs and changing skies of our Atlantic coastline and have been used by well-known international designer Giorgio Armani for his winter collection. Ready-made jackets, skirts, coats and hats can be bought throughout the country but it is Co Donegal, in the far north-west of the island, that boasts the best tweeds in the land. Here techniques in weaving have remained essentially the same since the time of the Celts. The 19th century saw the introduction of the fly shuttle loom into very popular use all along the western seaboard. Today, handweaving has survived in Co Donegal due to companies like McGee's of Donegal town and McNutts of Downings both of whom have operated very successful systems where the prepared warp beams are delivered to the weavers working throughout the countryside, and at the same time the previous week's woven tweed is collected for washing and finishing in the woollen mill. Donegal tweed is to be considered an investment buy and within the domain of woven goods there is a wealth of stoles and gossamer light rugs or 'throws' which can be used for different purposes - over the shoulders, on tables, over chairs to add a pool of light to a dark corner. Prestige tweed labels are available in any good department or specialist store throughout the country.

Like weaving, the history of spinning wool is a long one in Ireland. Today within sight and sound of the wild Atlantic Ocean, many spinning wheels turn rhythmically in time to the high lonely cry of the sandpiper, echoing the history of a craft which may go back 3,000 years into Ireland's past.

Natural Aran sweaters are generally made from wool of lowland Galway sheep while the coarser wool of the blackface sheep is used mainly for carpet making, blending and often for Donegal homespuns.

Handknitting is a craft with roots deep in the life of the Irish countryside. Handknit sweaters, caps, stockings, trousers and shawls were once commonly worn but the 'cottage industry' of Irish handknits has lasted longest along the western seaboard. The hand-knit sweaters of Donegal and the Aran Islands are world famous, made of heavy oiled wool. Guaranteed to keep out wind and weather, they are the traditional costume of the fisherman. Equipped with sweaters, homespun bawneen trousers and jackets, he braved the stormiest of seas in his traditional boat, the Currach. It was said that if a fisherman were drowned at sea and washed ashore far from home he might be identified by the stitches or pattern of his sweater or jacket.

The playwright, John Millington Synge, who based some of his most famous plays on the stories he had heard and the life he had experienced on the Aran Islands, described in "Riders to the Sea" how a girl identified the body of her drowned fisherman brother by the stocking he wore. 'It's the second of the third pair I knitted, and I put up three score stitches and I dropped four of them'.

In places like Aran and Donegal they will tell you that the stitches in a sweater have a meaning or tell a story relating to the life of the fisherman - sea, earth, sky, marriages,

2

1 Irish glass blowing - care and quality. *Photo: Daniel de Chenu*
2 Weaving - a long rural tradition. *Photo: Bord Failte*
3 Crafts in abundance. *Photo: Bord Failte*

sons to take his place. Many too, are supposed to have a religious significance. The Trinity (also known as the blackberry stitch) is supposed to represent the Holy Trinity. It is done by making three stitches from one, and one from three. The marriage lines or crooked road is a zig-zag stitch depicting the ups and downs of married life. Today the old and young women of Aran and Donegal still knit for their menfolk by hand in the same way their ancestors did in years gone by. Luckily for us, Aran and traditional knitwear can now be purchased almost anywhere and are available in shades that reflect the colours of the Irish countryside. Machine knits are also available but handknits, though more expensive, are a worthwhile buy.

Apart from traditional style handknits, one should also look out for the marvellously stylish and exotic knits of designers like Margaret Joyce, Glynis Robins and Lainey Keogh, along with Michelina Stacpoole (an Italian married to an Irishman) who have put young Irish designers on the map. Designer sweaters and cardigans are usually in linen or cotton. Also worth noting is the fact that cashmere is available in Ireland at prices much more competitive than on the continent.

Ireland produces some of the finest linen in the world. Its modern use gives us suits and skirts, jackets and shirts in subtle and natural shades. Its most famous exponent is internationally known Irish designer Paul Costelloe, a favourite of Princess Diana's. Costelloe's collections also demonstrate what wonderful things can be done with tweed and wool.

Linen has a long history in Ireland. Early literature has splendid descriptions of kings and queens, brave warriors and fair maidens wearing gowns and tunics of the finest linen. The present day methods of spinning wool and flax are broadly similar to those used in earliest times. Flax in fact was probably grown in Ireland from the Bronze Age onwards.

In the 17th century more than 6,000 flax wheels were introduced into the Donegal area alone, thus changing the social pattern of the countryside. As the wheel was light in weight it was easily transportable and it became customary for young women of the parish to gather in a different house each night for communal spinning. When work was done, all the young men of the locality would gather and the night ended with a dance.

Although the linen industry is centred mainly

in the counties of Ulster, articles can be purchased throughout the whole country. Novel ideas for the use of linen and which make ideal gifts are table cloths, napkins and placemats, as well as 'throws' for evening wear.

Another quality Irish-made product which makes an ideal gift is hand-made antique Irish lace from Limerick and Carrickmacross and mostly of the 19th century. Irish lace is internationally renowned and today throughout Ireland one can buy beautiful pieces of hand-made lace to use as tablecloths and place mats as well as ladies' gloves and collars. Every known method of making lace by hand has been used in Ireland at some time or other and in the 18th and 19th centuries the lace industry was seen as the handmaid of agriculture. Lace making in the home was not an integral part of native vernacular culture but was introduced so that large families living on small uneconomic land holdings could remain there. The making of lace was executed by women and girls who, once trained, practiced at home.

Training in lace making was given free of charge at lace schools of which a countrywide network sprang up in the middle and latter years of the 19th century with Limerick and Carrickmacross becoming the more famous techniques. Irish lace making suffered badly during the First World War and unfortunately never regained a firm foothold. However today we see a revival of this particular cottage industry as Carrickmacross and crochet lace are produced for haute couture and the tourist trade, with individuals sometimes making it for their own use.

Another housewifely skill which occupies a special place in Irish craft tradition is patchwork and on display in some of the best specialist and craft shops in the country are marvellous bed quilts, cushion covers and picnic spreads in the most original designs using plain as well as printed fabrics. Elaborate patterns combining squares and triangles in cotton or silk make the most impressive and creative patchwork and prove to be ideal gifts with a distinctly Irish look.

Moving away from the clothes and fabrics scene once again, we find that Ireland offers countless ideas for gifts in glass, silver and gold, perfumes and pottery all with a unique Irish look, feel or smell.

Irish crystal from Waterford, Cavan, Galway and Tyrone is created by some of the best master blowers in the world using traditional methods and appreciating in value with time. Irish crystal is a gift to value and treasure.

Glass making or more correctly, full lead crystal, would seem an oddly exotic art for a remotely situated, agricultural country not blessed with abundant mineral resources. To go beyond the mere availability of materials to the mystique which has grown around Irish crystal (Waterford in particular) is to encapsulate a thousand years of Irish history including the arrival of the Celts who brought with them their artistry in metalwork. There was much gold and copper but no precious stones, so, to highlight their delicate artifacts they used the millefiori methods of fusing glass rods to make jewel-like inserts.

Later on, under the reign of Elizabeth I, various entrepreneurs were given patents to set up glasshouses in Ireland and the first such premises recorded is still known as Curryglass, not far from Dungarvan where Waterford Glass now has its second factory. In the centuries that followed Irish craftsmen were renowned for their precision and excellence in the art of glass cutting, revealing an amazing depth of artistry. By the early 18th century, Waterford glass had achieved such

fame that it was now sparkling on the tables of American connoisseurs and in the West Indies. The art of glass blowing has changed very little in the past two hundred years and a lot of preparation goes into the finished product which is blown, engraved and cut by the artist craftsmen. A comparatively small amount of Waterford crystal is engraved as it is a technique requiring great patience, skillful fingers and excellent eyesight. As a spin-off to the success of Waterford, a number of glass factories including Cavan, Tyrone and Galway are now producing excellent items which make memorable gifts. Irish crystal is on sale in department and specialist Irish stores throughout the country. Other Irish glass to look for includes Kerry glass in Killarney making tiny

3

colourful and ornamental objects, Paschal Fitzpatrick specialising in decorative glass at the crafts centre, Strokestown, Co Roscommon and Jerpoint Glass in Co Kilkenny.

No visitor should return home without casting an eye over the marvellous collection of antique and contemporary gold and silver picture frames, cutlery and of course jewellery that are available in Ireland. Irish silver, particularly Georgian, is world famous and even if you do not wish to buy a large piece there are some smaller items such as spoons, salt cellars, milk and cream jugs as well as snuff boxes that make elegant and unusual gifts. Modern silver jewellery made by specialist artists using traditional methods as well as very innovative designs makes a distinctive buy. Traditional jewellery with Celtic motifs is enjoying something of a comeback as more young Irish people discover the art and pleasure of jewellery making. Some interesting pieces to look out for are Ogham Crafts silver moone cross and Celtic bracelets as well as Kevin O'Dwyer's silver range. The Tara range of Celtic crosses and brooches as well as the Book of Kells designs are all worth looking at.

An interesting piece of Irish jewellery which has a fascinating tale is the claddagh ring. In the form of two hands holding a heart surmounted by a crown, it belongs to a class known as 'fede' rings from medieval times and was adopted as a betrothal and marriage ring by the people of Claddagh, a fishing village near Galway city in the west of the island. That village no longer exists, but its people who had their own "king" and "queen' are remembered world wide by their ring. Reproduced in gold and silver, the motif of hands and heart is used for earrings and pendants which, though pretty, are not as authentic as the rings. The symbol is also repeated in Galway crystal.

To bring a touch of 'Irishness' to your kitchen, take home some of the wonderful earthenware produced by professional Irish potters and available all over the country. The last decade has seen a revival in what is one of the country's most ancient crafts. As a result, one has an incredible choice of chunky traditional designs such as Shangarry pottery. More innovative and new designs are by McCluskey and the 'Matisse' range by Tom Agnew. Other names to look out for are Louis

Mulcahy in Kerry, Rossmore in West Cork and Mosse and Jackson in Kilkenny. Their wares are found in many of the top quality craft shops located all over Ireland.

A delicate contrast to all the robust pottery is the fineware of Belleek and Royal Tara. Belleek's porcelain has won major awards, art critics acclaim and influential patronage and is available in various ornamental yet delicate designs. Royal Tara, which operates out of Galway, produces fine bona china and its range includes beautiful dinner services, exquisite mantle clocks, ornate table lamp bases, pretty vases and delicate tankards. Also worth looking out for is the Carrigaline pottery range of inexpensive domestic earthenware, souvenirs and art pottery as well as the Arklow Pottery Co Ltd which produces a similar range.

Other lovely gift ideas are the National Gallery canvas reproductions of old masters like Walter Osborne's Apple Picking and Thomas Gainsborough's The Cottage Girl, along with tapestry cushions and Royal Irish silk ties, hand painted plates, especially the Elaine Murphy

5

4 Irish cheese - a successful blend of quality natural resources and recently acquired skills.
Photo: Anro Graphic Studio Ltd.

5 Irish lace - labour of love. *Photo: Bord Failte*

Celtic series featuring Irish myths and legends. Why not bring home some Irish sounds on cassette, LP or CD. Some of the more famous Irish musicians include: Clannad, The Chieftains, The Dubliners, Enya, U2, Sinead O'Connor, The Pogues and Van Morrison.

Novel small souvenirs that can easily be carried include linen tea towels printed in pretty and witty designs, golfing hats made from tweed, posters showing Irish castles, cottages, pubs as well as the Georgian doorways of Dublin, not to mention the more comical one of the guy dressed in his welly boots exposing himself to a herd of cows entitled "Expose yourself to Ireland". How about some Irish perfume or soap? Fresh smells that endure memories of the Irish countryside. A number of new types have been produced by very innovative young Irish people and are available in specialist stores.

Getting on to tastier topics, one must not forget the fact that Ireland boasts the best smoked salmon in the world and once you have had an opportunity to savour this delicious delicacy then you will understand why the rich and famous have it flown specially to their tables. Vacuum packed, oak-smoked salmon is the ultimate taste of Ireland and makes an ideal gift. Available throughout the country at prices ranging from £16.50 - £19.50 per kg. It is possible to call in on many of the local fisheries preparing smoked salmon and watch some of the process taking place. Fresh water or wild Atlantic salmon are used for smoking, thus ensuring the finest quality.

To wash it all down why not treat yourself to a bottle of the 'hard stuff' or as you might know it, whiskey. Whiskey or 'uisce beatha' (water of life) is the Irishman's favourite spirit. Pure Irish barley and crystal-clear water are the ingredients that go into making this the gentlest, mellowest of all whiskeys. Part of the barley used is malted and then dried in closed kilns and not over open peat fires. Thus 'Irish' does not have a smokey taste. It is distilled three times so that the utmost purity is achieved and the ideal balance of taste elements is retained. The new whiskey is then put away in oak casks to mature in dark, cool warehouses for anything between seven and twelve years. Some of the great names to look out for are Jameson, Black Bush, Old Bushmills, Paddy, Tullamore Dew, Powers and Crested Ten. Other nice Irish drinks are Baileys, a liquor made from original Irish cream and whiskey...delicious when served on the rocks, and Irish Mist, another equally good liquor made from whiskey. They make ideal gifts. Drink up, then and choose your favourite. Slainté!

If you decide to take home some more 'tastes' of Ireland, then why not try out some of the top-quality homemade cheeses that are sold all over the country. There are approximately 40 Irish farmhouse cheesemakers all producing excellent cheeses that vary from the delicate to the more pungent. Some of the favourites include Glen o Sheen, a traditional farmhouse cheddar available in red or white, Ardrahan, a semi-soft Gouda-type made in Co Cork, Emerald Irish Brie made in Co Wexford, Cooleeney Camembert, a cheese with a semi-

liquid interior and a pronounced flavour made in Co Tipperary, and Cashel Blue, also made in Co Tipperary. The Irish cheese industry has come a long way in the past decade when the general demand was for processed cheeses. With the home market's demand for home made cheeses increasing, and the recognition of Irish cheese on the continent becoming steadily greater, things are looking good.

Other home produced goods that make novel gifts include the traditional porter cake made from Guinness. Tasty homemade jams, pure Wexford honey, Irish whiskey marmalade, homemade fudge and handmade chocolates filled with delicious liquors such as Baileys or Irish Mist. All to be savoured and simply a culinary experience!

During your stay in Ireland, you may notice that the Irish do love their tea and good tea at that! Bewleys Oriental Cafes in Dublin and their branches in other cities are a must if you wish to buy not just a good ordinary tea but varieties such as Darjeeling, Keemun, LapSang Suchong and many others. Very popular with most tourists is the idea of bringing home a tea pot from Ireland, so do not miss your chance of buying a homely china one from Bewleys or other stores.

So you see, it's not easy to leave Ireland empty-handed, such is the choice and quality of home-produced goods that have a distinct Irish trademark to them. Throughout the country you will find a good network of retail outlets for quality Irish products and although shopping is made simple by the availability of these goods in specialist city stores, half the fun can be in discovering the goodies in some off the beaten track craft shop miles from nowhere.

Happy hunting!.

Colette Dennison is a freelance journalist and guide who has worked extensively in Ireland and Italy. She presently resides in the historic town of Kells, Co Meath.

IRELAND,
an ecologist's dream ?

Michael Viney

1

From my home on Ireland's rugged
west coast, I look out to a whole shoal
of islands adrift in the bay between Mayo
and Connemara. A couple of them are
substantial enough to have a little harbour
for fishing boats, and hay meadows,
church and school. Two others hold the
ruins of ancient Christian settlements
and the bee-hive cells of monks.
The rest are small, rocky fragments, fringed
with foam, and are the refuges of seals
and otters and the summer colonies
of seabirds.

As an islander, I love even smaller islands, each with its own special feeling of containment and seclusion. To visit any of them is a pilgrimage, but sometimes with an undercurrent of concern: will anything happen to spoil the island - will it be the same next time? Ireland, too, has become a place of pilgrimage, as continental Europeans seek out its distinctive natural atmosphere. The foundations for it were created some 7,500 years ago, when the Atlantic Ocean swirled in to isolate the final outpost of Europe. The island remains ecologically special, its natural heritage largely untouched by the pressures of industry or population. But will anything happen to spoil it? Conserving the image of Ireland as Europe's cleanest, greenest country is a difficult challenge for a people short of jobs and income.

What makes its ecology so special?

Size for size, few pieces of the earth's crust offer such a jig-saw of ancient rocks or support such a wide range of natural habitats. Variety, too, keeps Ireland green. Swift changes of mild ocean weather send showers and sunshine across the countryside to nourish an abundance of wildflowers.

For almost two millions years, however, the island was either ice-covered or was a cold, bleak

1 An ancient and intact landscape, Dingle Penninsula, Co. Kerry .
Photo: Jole Bortoli
2 Irish sheep at home in the landscape.
Photo: Jole Bortoli
3 Bird sanctuary in the city - Booterstown, Dublin.
Photo: Jole Bortoli

desert. The glaciers carved the walls of the mountains, and their final retreat, 10,000 years ago, left Ireland fretted with hundreds of sparkling lakes. Later, a period of cool, moist climate helped to create the most distinctive feature of the Irish countryside - the great, rolling vistas of peatland, covered in heather, mosses and colourful bog-plants.

On the lowlands of Ireland, bogs grew up from ancient, shallow lakes; on the western hills, the peatland formed as a blanket, sometimes metres thick, smothering the stumps of ancient pines. Once scorned as wasteland, fit only for digging as fuel, the surviving Irish bogs are now recognised as a precious and fascinating ecosystem long vanished from most of western Europe.

When Ireland was finally cut off by sea, many of the plants, birds and animals moving northwards after the ice age had still not colonised the island, so it has fewer species than neighbouring Britain. But the undisturbed character of much of the countryside brings wildlife together and makes it easier to see.

Aside from the "wilderness" areas of bog and mountain, the Irish landscape is mainly green and pastoral, with large areas - especially in the west - in which the patchwork of small fields has changed little in a hundred years. The field walls of Connacht and the western islands are crusted with slow-growing lichens that confirm the purity of the Atlantic air.

Inland, the fields are bounded by hedgerows, and this intricate network of hawthorn bushes and small trees - a sort of linear woodland - provides shelter for nesting songbirds: thrush and robin, wren and blackbird, and many more. The fields and hillsides give cover to larks and pipits and migrant wheatears. Unlike countries such as Italy and France, there is no tradition of shooting small birds for food, and the countryside chorus of jubilant birdsong is one of the pleasures of the spring.

Because Ireland is predominantly a grass and cattle economy, with tillage crops confined to the drier south and east, the use of pesticides and herbicides has been far lower than in the rest of Europe. There are no "prairie" regions of hedgeless arable land, constantly sprayed with chemicals. Insect life is still rich and well-balanced and this, too, helps to keep the land a nourishing habitat for birds and bats, hedgehogs and shrews.

But an island full of cattle has other impacts on nature. Most farmland was once "unimproved" permanent pasture, made up of native grasses and other herbiage. The meadows mown for hay were full of wildflowers, bees and butterflies. Steadily, over recent decades, this vegetation has changed. The standard field-sward is now based on the lusher Italian rye-grass, maintained to a vivid, uniform green by nitrate fertilizer.

In the areas of richer farmland, wildflowers and butterflies are now banished to the hedgerows and the verges of country lanes. But on the poorer land of the west, on the islands and along the Shannon, old, moist meadows still survive, glowing in early summer with purple orchids, ragged robin and marsh marigold.

It was the intensification of livestock farming that made Ireland's first ecological problems. Animal slurries polluted several prime angling lakes and rivers, and huge nation-wide investment has been made to help farmers keep the effluents from silage and livestock out of their local streams. This has worked remarkably well in most parts, so that herons still fish in the quiet rural waterways, and otters swim by night beneath the bridges of large country towns.

But farming can still conflict with particular species. For example, the campaign to eradicate disease from Ireland's cattle herds has prompted persecution of the badger, blamed for spreading bovine TB. Although protected by law, badgers, like foxes, may now be safer living at the edges of cities than in the countryside.

The switch from traditional hay-making to silage is threatening the survival of the corncrake, a migrant rail from Africa that has already disappeared from most of Europe. The earlier mowing of meadows destroys its nests and young, and the bird's mysterious call, once familiar on summer nights all over Ireland, is now confined to small areas of the north-west and on the water-meadows of the River Shannon.

Broad and slow-flowing, the Shannon drains the heartland of Ireland. In winter, floods spill over its banks and thousands of hectares become an important wetland for ducks, geese and waders flying in form the Arctic and eastern Europe. Ireland's wetlands and estuaries offer wintering grounds for huge migrant flocks and are vital to their survival. Although shooting is closely regulated in Ireland, and most species of birds are totally protected, there is recurrent controversy about the wisdom of promoting shooting as a tourist attraction. Italian and French shooting parties, in particular, are sometimes resented by Irish hunters, who fear over-exploitation of gamebirds such as snipe and woodcock.

Most Irish farms are small - less than 50 hectares - and almost all are still owned by individual families. However inefficient this may seem economically, it has helped Ireland to avoid the kind of ecological damage that often goes with farming on a larger, more commercial scale. There is, however, an inexorable drift from the land, and many small farmers are pessimistic

of land in Ireland's most beautiful and ecologically sensitive areas.

The pressures of colonial history left Ireland as one of the least forested countries of Europe (5 per cent of land under trees, compared with Italy's 21 per cent) and the government now wants to double the rate of planting to 30,000 hectares a year in 1993. Many of the new trees will be on marginal farmland, and there are special incentives for planting broadleafed trees such as oak and ash, but conservationists fear a further spread of conifer forests across the peatland of the west.

Plantations of fast-growing spruce and pine already cover the slopes of many of Connacht's mountains. The result is sometimes attractively "alpine", but most connoisseurs of landscape prefer the distinctive wildness of the untouched bog. In rugged Connemara, the conifers are being blamed for making the water too acid in some of the region's treasured trout and salmon streams. This is puzzling, because the rain that falls on these forests is probably the cleanest and least acid in Europe. Scientists are working on the problem.

They have also been studying another ecological coincidence. The past few years have seen a dramatic expansion of fish-farming in the crystal-clear inlets of Ireland's Atlantic coast. In waters where the industry is most intense, there has been a sudden, catastrophic decline in the health of the native wild sea-trout. These are close relatives of the captive salmon, caged in great numbers in the bays where the sea-trout feed. Salmon farms are now widely mistrusted as a source of harm to more traditional fisheries, but research continues on ways to make them more acceptable.

After a century in which nothing very much happened to change the romantic and unspoiled character of Connacht, one momentous ecological development seems to follow on another. The first big

7

8

development seems to follow on another. The first big forestry plantations (partly financed by the European Investment Bank) were followed by EC subsidies on hill-sheep. These have helped to produce such overgrazing of the rain-washed hills that in a few places they are now eroding to bare rocks. After the fish-cages comes discovery of gold, in apparently large and commercial quantities, in the mountains of County Mayo.

One major find was in the peak of Croagh Patrick, hallowed since ancient times as a "holy" mountain and the scene of Ireland's most famous Catholic pilgrimage. Fierce public protest at the prospect of a mine brought a government decision to halt the project - and a huge claim for compensation from the mining company. But exploratory drilling continues a few miles further south, at a big gold-bearing zone which straddles Doolough Pass, one of Connacht's most scenic mountain valleys.

Tourism itself creates ecological pressures, as local development groups look for ways to attract more visitors. At times,

the "improvements" they conceive can threaten the very environment that tourists find appealing. In Connemara, for example, local interests have been pressing to build an airport on part of a prime wilderness area of peatland and lakes. The experience of solitude and freedom from man-made noise, while deeply valued by visitors from crowded countries, may enjoy little appreciation in the remoter communities in Ireland.

While the country has a well-developed system of physical planning and control of development, there is no national policy to fix the priorities of land-

use - between, say, forest and wilderness, or mining and tourism. There is, indeed, a list of "areas of Scientific Interest", ranked by national and international importance, but this has not always guaranteed ecological protection, and conservation seems constantly under siege.

At the heart of many problems is the question of compensation - whether citizens should be paid when they lose the right to sell their land for commercial forests or airports or tourist developement. Ireland cannot afford to spend huge amounts of money on compensation, or on buying land to set aside as national parks.

So what is to be done to conserve the island's most "natural" landscapes, which are owned, as a rule, by the country's poorest people? The EC has offered one answer in its scheme of Environmentally Sensitive Areas, (ESAs). This pays farmers an annual subsidy to continue with traditional, environment-friendly, farming methods - to leave hay-meadows "unimproved", for example, and keep stock numbers low, or to leave wetlands undrained for winter wildfowl. The idea has been officially adopted by the Irish Government as part of a new "environment action programme". But it cannot be used very widely if the cost is to fall on Ireland alone.

Almost the whole of the western seaboard could be considered an Environmentally Sensitive Area and this is where many Dutch, Germans and French have built their second homes. If Ireland is to provide Europe's "unspoiled" natural playground, the EC may have to help in keeping it that way.

Meanwhile, new legislation for "heritage areas" will introduce more control of sensitive landscapes. New national parks are to take shape in the Wicklow Mountains, south of Dublin, and in the dramatic, botanically-rich limestone hills of the Burren, Co

Clare, and these will add to those already created in Kerry, Connemara and Donegal. The national nature reserves already include several important pieces of peatland, but the area of completely unspoiled bog is dwindling year by year.

What will happen to the farming landscape of Ireland has never seemed more uncertain, as the continuity of familiar agricultural patterns is challenged by economic change. A flight of farmers from the land could lead to much bigger farms in far fewer hands, and the spread of more intensive and ecologically harmful methods. The promotion of organic farming, on the other hand, already funded by the government, could help to give Ireland's "green" image a new reality on the ground.

How seriously committed the government is to its Environment Action Programme will be tested by events. For example, all sewage pollution of inland waters and untreated discharge from major coastal towns is due to end by the year 2000, after investment of more than £600 million. Ireland's generous supply of totally unpolluted water has been one of the island's biggest assets in attracting the pharmaceutical plants that, with electronics, now lead its industrial development.

Despite some 25 years in which multi-national companies setting up in Ireland have largely been left to police their own performance on pollution, Ireland has been remarkably free from serious toxic incidents. One important episode, in which farmland was poisoned by incinerator fumes from a pharmaceutical factory, did, however, produce vehement public concern which disrupted the recruitment of further chemical plants to "green field" sites in the countryside. Planning conditions are now more elaborate and stringent, and a new Environmental Protection Agency, long overdue, will monitor the industries' compliance.

Indeed, for a country which, only a few years ago, was bottom of the European league in environmental concern, Ireland has caught up on the "green" revolution with surprising speed and vigour. In a country so handicapped by unemployment and emigration, there might well have been a willingness to make more jobs at any cost. It hasn't happened, and will not happen now. The Irish, too, enjoy living in what is still - if more, perhaps, by chance than judgment - the cleanest country in Europe.

9 A sea of bogcotten. *Photo: Douglas*
10 Traditional turf cutting in the Wicklow mountains .*Photo: Jole Bortoli*

Michael Viney, formerly Environment Correspondent of the Irish Times, now writes a weekly column in that newspaper, on wildlife and ecolological affairs, from his home on the coast of County Mayo.

Overview
social and political
Liam McAuley

The early 1990s are proving to be a time of both hope and confusion for the Republic of Ireland. On the positive side, the country managed in the late 1980's to shake off the economic paralysis and stagnation of the previous few years to achieve impressive economic growth and a healthy trading surplus. Its people began the 1990s by electing their first woman President and committing themselves to a unified Europe (approving the Treaty of Maastricht by a two-to-one majority in a referendum).

Yet its politicians have failed to tackle deep social and economic problems – high unemployment and emigration, disturbing social inequality – or to give leadership on issues of personal rights, such as divorce and abortion. They have also been undermined and distracted by a series of financial scandals that reinforced widespread suspicions about dubious links between businessmen and politicians. Meanwhile, the seemingly insoluble conflict in Northern Ireland – which has claimed more than 3,000 lives in the past 23 years – refuses to go away, like a mad relation in the upstairs bedroom whom the family tries to ignore.

The past two years have been marked by a series of political shocks that no one could have expected at the start of 1991. The leader of the populist Fianna Fail party, Charles Haughey – the dominant personality in Irish politics since the mid-1970s – had enjoyed a charmed period since his return to power in 1987 at the head of a minority government. With the co-operation of the main opposition party, Fine Gael – whose leader decided to suspend normal political hostilities in the interests of the shaky economy – Haughey had implemented tough public spending cuts to curb inflation, reduce interest rates and control the state's mountainous foreign debt.

The treatment was painful – especially for poorer people, as public health and housing services bore the brunt of the cuts – but it worked. Trade unions agreed to wage restraint in the national interest, business confidence returned and investment flowed in from American, Japanese and European companies attracted by generous tax incentives. As exports boomed, the economy grew in 1989 and 1990 by around 7 per cent a year – over twice the average rate for EC countries. By 1991, the external payment surplus reached 6.7 per cent of gross national output. Perhaps the most obvious sign of greater affluence was the property boom of 1988-1990, which saw the average price of a house in Dublin jump from under £40,000 to over £60,000 (average salaries rose from £12,000 to £20,000).

But in spite of the expansion, unemployment continued to rise. More jobs were being provided, but not nearly enough to cope with the flood of young people on to the labour market as a result of the high birth rates of the 1960s and 1970s. The average number of children per family has fallen to about 2.1 compared with 4 in 1971.

Better times brought popularity for the Government and its leader, but there were some signs that Haughey's golden touch was deserting him. In 1989 he called a general election in an ill-judged attempt to win the overall parliamentary majority that had eluded him throughout his career. But his party Fianna Fail returned from the polls

Above: Mary Robinson, first female President of the Republic. Photo: Derek Speirs/Report
Below: Leaders of the main political parties outside Dail Eireann. Photo: Eamonn Farrell.

with fewer seats rather than more and Haughey was forced into coalition – ironically with the centre-right Progressive Democrats, founded in 1986 by former Fianna Fail members disaffected by Haughey's leadership.

In 1990, his party's candidate for President (a largely symbolic role) was sensationally defeated by the left-wing candidate Mary Robinson, a leading lawyer and feminist. Still, as 1991 opened, an opinion poll showed a remarkable 60 per cent of the electorate was happy with the Government. Haughey agreed a "Programme for Economic and Social Progress" with the unions, employers and farmers and hailed it, with characteristic hyperbole, as the envy of Europe, "the most comprehensive agreement of its kind, covering all economic and social areas".

Freedom to choose – Irish women demonstrate on the ferry to England.
Photo: Eamonn Farrell

The 'Haughey Era' Ends

But that summer and autumn the media uncovered a series of business scandals. A TV investigation of the giant Goodman meat processing concern made allegations of malpractice, tax evasion and political favoritism, especially in the granting of generous export insurance (against creditors defaulting on debts). After a furious parliamentary row, Haughey announced a public judicial inquiry into the affair. The press revealed that directors of the state-controlled sugar company (now privatised) had lined their own pockets by dealing in shares and that the chairman of the state telecommunications company had been part-owner of a site later bought by the company at a hefty profit to the vendors. The huge sums of money mentioned seemed the more grotesque by contrast with the ever-lengthening dole queues as unemployment neared 20 per cent. While Haughey had no proven involvement in any of these affairs, he was damaged because of his apparent friendship with some of the central figures and because his own conspicuous but unexplained personal wealth left him liable to be deemed guilty by association. As discontent grew, he survived a leadership challenge within his party that autumn (1991), but was forced from office early in the New Year and replaced by Albert Reynolds, his former minister for industry and commerce.

Anti abortion demonstrators march in Dublin.
Photo: Derek Speirs/Report

Reynolds, a homelier figure with none of Haughey's charisma, began by promising to "open the windows and let in the air". But the shadow of scandal continued to haunt the Government, not least because Reynolds had been a central figure in the events being investigated in the beef tribunal. Reynolds also seemed determined to snub and humiliate Progressive Democrat members of the Government.

If his intention was to goad them into resignation, causing a general election, his wish was fulfilled in dramatic fashion: appearing at the tribunal Reynolds accused the PD leader, Desmond O'Malley, of being dishonest in earlier sworn testimony. The implied charge of perjury was too much for the long suffering PD's and they withdrew from the Government forcing a general election on November 25th.

Disgusted with having a general election forced upon them, the people of Ireland blamed Reynolds and his Fianna Fail party for the upheavals they were facing and at the polls some of the party's loyal supporters gave their votes to Labour and other parties. Outgoing Fianna Fail suffered the worst defeat in 65 years, losing 10 seats. The triumphant Labour party celebrated its best election since 1918. It won an extra 17 seats – bringing its total to 33 and making it the major power broker in the formation of the new Government in coalition with Fianna Fail. This new and unlikely coalition has been formed with a radical new programme for government.

The Abortion Debate

On the same day that the Irish people were asked to vote in a general election they were also asked to adjudicate by referendum on a bizarre debate about abortion which had ensnared the Fianna Fail/PD Government for much of 1992. The controversy had erupted earlier that year, soon after Albert Reynolds took office. It emerged that the attorney-general, the Government's chief advisor, had sought an injunction to prevent a 14-year-old alleged rape victim having an abortion in England. He had become aware of the case after the girl's parents had asked police investigating whether tissue from an aborted foetus could be used forensically to establish the identity of the rapist.

The roots of the affair went back to

1983, when anti-abortion campaigners forced the Government to hold a referendum to amend the Consitution so that abortion could not be made legal in the Republic.

To many people, the proposal seemed both hypocritical and irrelevant since an estimated 4,000 Irish women travel to Britain each year for abortions. But after a vitriolic public debate, the proposal was carried and the Constitution was amended to say that: *"The State acknowledges the right to life of the unborn and, with due regard to the equal right to life of the mother, guarantees in its laws to respect and, as far as practicable, by its laws to defend and vindicate that right."* (Article 40.3.3.). The attorney-general, having been made aware of the 14-year-old's planned abortion, now felt himself obliged, as guardian of the Constitution, to intervene. To the horror of everyone, a High Court judge upheld the injunction and forbade the girl and her family to leave the country for 10 months.

Bizarrely, the Government now found itself privately pleading with the family to appeal the case to the Supreme Court (final arbiter of the Constitution) and openly offering to pay the costs of the appeal.

In the midst of intense controversy and recrimination, the Supreme Court allowed the appeal – not, as expected, on the basis of EC law guaranteeing free movement between states, but because the court judged that Article 40.3.3. permitted abortion where there was a real and substantial risk to the life of the mother, in this case, from suicide (according to psychological evidence). In other words, the 1983 amendment meant that abortion was now legal in Ireland – exactly the reverse of what the proponents had intended.

Undeterred, anti-abortion groups, supported by the Catholic bishops, demanded that the people should be

Irish unemployment has now soared to over 300,000, the highest in the E.C. Unemployed demonstrate in Dublin.   Photo: Eamonn Farrell

New found popularity for the Labour Party who won 33 seats in the recent General Election.   Photo: Eamonn Farrell.

given another vote on the matter. The Government acceded, partly to avoid that summer's referendum on the Treaty of Maastricht being stymied by a protest vote; but it cannily delayed publishing its exact proposals until the Maastricht poll was safely out of the way.

In the event, three proposals were put to the electorate. The first guaranteed freedom of travel (thereby ensuring that women could continue to go abroad for abortion). The second promised freedom of information "relating to services lawfully available in another state". The third, and most contentious, outlawed termination of pregnancy unless it was necessary to save the life, "as distinct from the health, of the mother". It also specifically excluded the risk of suicide which had been acknowledged by the Supreme Court.

"Pro-life" groups protested angrily that voters should have the option of a total ban on abortion within the state. "Pro-choice" campaigners objected to the dubious and derogatory distinction between a woman's "life and health"; to the disregard for mental health implied in the exclusion of a suicide risk; and to the fact that the Government had opted to hold a referendum rather than to legislate on the basis of the Supreme Court's interpretations of Article 40.3.3.

As it transpired, the first two proposals were passed by the Irish electorate, but the most contentious substantive issue was overturned by a two to one majority, thus leaving in place the Supreme Court ruling on the matter. It is inevitable, however, that the 1992 referendum will further fuel a debate with crucial implications for the future role of the Catholic Church in Irish society and, above all, for the status of women. Perhaps the most striking feature of the abortion debate was that it was carried on by powerful cliques – politicians, lawyers, clerics, doctors – consisting overwhelmingly of men.

Ireland's lost youth

If women struggle to be heard in the centres of power, so also do the young. Outside observers of the Irish scene in recent years have often predicted social upheaval. With nearly half the population under 25, and no prospect of a solution to the unemployment crisis, surely some great explosion is inevitable? But none has come – principally because of the safety valve of emigration, a constant factor in Irish society for the past 150 years.

More to the point, perhaps, is the fatalism with which young people emigrate – at a rate of some 30,000 per year – mainly to Britain and the United States. Apart from the need to work, they talk of being forgotten by "the system". They see little point in staying at home struggling to change society. "That is no country for old men" the poet W.B. Yeats wrote of the Ireland of the 1920s. The great sadness today is that so many of the younger members of Europe's youngest population feel it is no country for the young.

Civil War politics

It is easy enough to see why they should feel that politics has little relevance for them: the raisons d'etre of the two dominant parties are to be found, not in any great ideological differences, but in the vicious Civil War that split the newly independent state after the 1921 Treaty with Britain. Under the Treaty, the country was divided into what is now the Republic with the six northern counties remaining under English rule.

The pro-Treaty side won the civil war at a Pyrrhic cost to the new state. The Fine Gael party was founded by supporters of the Treaty, Fianna Fail by its opponents. But it was Fianna Fail which won the peace, and its founder, Eamon de Valera, who went on to become the father figure of independent Ireland, becoming Taoiseach from 1932 until 1948 (and from 1951 to 1954 and 1957-1959). He also introduced the state's

Poverty – an everyday part of Irish life. Photo: Eamonn Farrell

Constitution in 1937. The Ireland which de Valera ruled and personified was fiercely independent, rural, agricultural and pious (publications and films were strictly censored). It was also poor, economically protectionist, and industrially backward.

After Sean Lemass succeeded De Valera as Fianna Fail leader and Taoiseach in 1958, he launched a major programme of economic expansion which effectively

The referendum on Maastricht was a bitter battle but the Irish voted 2:1 to ratify the treaty. Photo: Eamonn Farrell.

took his country into the modern era. Priority was given to export industries and tax incentives were used to attract foreign investment (still a major plank in Irish economic strategy). Socially too, Ireland became more liberal, sharing in the "youth revolution" of the 1960s. But as the decade ended, the unfinished business of partition came to the fore again as civil strife erupted in Northern Ireland.

Entry to the European Community was welcomed enthusiastically in 1973, for its obvious benefits for the country's farmers and because it allowed Ireland to emerge from the post-colonial shadow of Britain. High prices for cattle, sheep and dairy produce meant greater prosperity for farmers; but as the effects of the oil crisis became felt, industrial unemployment rose and inflation neared 25 per cent. There was increasing concern about excessive state spending in the creation of non-productive public service jobs. Jack Lynch, who had followed Lemass as Fianna Fail leader, resigned as Taoiseach in 1979, and the "Haughey era" began.

Its early years were marked by extraordinary political infighting and instability. At one stage in 1981-82, there were three elections within 18 months, Fianna Fail minority administrations alternating with Fine Gael-Labour coalitions led by Garret Fitzgerald. The last of these, from late 1982-87, succeeded in negotiating the Anglo-Irish Agreement, which gives the Irish Government some say in the administration of Northern Ireland.

Fitzgerald's coalition might also have introduced the fiscal discipline the Irish economy needed, but Labour could not agree to cuts in social and health budgets. Ironically, it was left to Haughey, who in opposition had obstructed FitzGerald's efforts at reform, to administer the necessary strong medicine.

Despite world recession and the recent turbulence in currency markets, the Irish economy is now in better shape to tackle the chronic problem of unemployment and the social ills that flow from it; poverty, homelessness, urban crime and drug abuse. But its politicians must find some way to build broad support for a careful and thorough strategy.

They must also stop squabbling and show leadership. Ireland is a country of great energy, but much of it is dissipated and frustrated. The three 'national aims' constantly reiterated by Eamon de Valera – reviving the Irish language, ending emigration and reuniting the island of Ireland – remain pious aspirations. Gaelic is in everyday use by fewer than 100,000 people in small pockets along the western seaboard; too many of the young still leave; and the violent legacy of partition is far from spent.

The country's leaders must re-examine these goals and frame new ones to galvanise a restless society. That is the challenge and the need of the 1990s.

Liam McAuley is an assistant editor of The Irish Times.

THE NORTH

THE PAST

Norman Mongan

The Battle of the Boyne – from the painting by Jan Wyck (1616-1677)
Courtesy: National Gallery of Ireland.

One of the first questions that visitors to Ireland ask is about the Northern 'troubles'. It is not easy to find a simple answer to such a complex issue, especially one so deeply rooted in Irish history. The international media have somewhat erroneously presented it as a religious conflict but the roots of the problem go back to the 16th century Tudor plantations when the English crown began a policy of settling Protestant 'planters' on the confiscated lands of resisting Gaelic clans. In an attempt to create a greater understanding of the problems that exist in Northern Ireland today, writer and historian Norman Mongan traces the course of Ulster's history from the Tudors in the 16th century to partition in the 1920's.

Ulster was an ancient Celtic kingdom ruled by the paramount O'Neill kings and their ancestors for centuries. It was a pastoral society where wealth and power were measured by the vast herds of cattle they grazed. By the 16th century Ulster remained the most Gaelic province where Anglo-Norman influence had hardly penetrated.

Following a policy started by Henry VIII after the Reformation, Queen Mary Tudor and her Spanish consort Philip undertook the plantation of Leinster on the eastern coast of Ireland. The confiscated lands were redistributed to Protestant English and Scottish planters. Elizabeth I, Henry's other daughter, continued the policy in Ulster where she had to deal with ongoing revolt led by the O'Neill's and the Northern chiefs.

On Christmas day 1601, after nine years of war, the combined forces of the O'Neills and their Spanish allies were crushed by Lord Mountjoy at the Battle of Kinsale. The lands of the rebel northern chieftains were confiscated and O'Neill and his followers were forced into exile in Rome. With the 'flight of the earls', Gaelic political power in Ireland came to an end.

The Crown's plantation policy in Ulster intensified as large numbers of Scottish planters settled bringing with them the stern and puritanical teachings of John Calvin.

The Catholic population's resentment smouldered until 1641 when there was a national uprising against the Protestant planters of Leinster and Ulster. Cromwell, the English Puritan leader, arrived in 1649 to quell the revolt, notable with the massacre of the total population of Drogheda. Irish resistance seemed definitely broken and from 1652 the remaining Catholic landowners were expropriated and forced west into the barren bogs of Connacht. The "Acts of Settlement" handed their lands over to Cromwellian officers and men in reward for their efforts.

The Battle of the Boyne

Catholic hopes were rekindled with the restoration of a Catholic royalty in 1662. James II abolished the 'Acts of Settlement' and a few Catholic landowners did regain their property. By 1689 however, James had been dethroned by his Protestant son-in-law, William of Orange and Ireland became their battleground when James, in vain, laid siege to Derry. In 1690 James suffered a terrible defeat at the battle of the Boyne and with the Treaty of Limerick, signed a year later, James and his followers were forced into exile in France. To this day, Ulster's Orangemen ritually celebrate their victory at the Battle of the Boyne, every July 12th.

Civil rights and religious liberties were stripped of the Catholic population by a series of penal laws introduced between 1695 and 1727. They could no longer vote or buy land and only the lowest occupations were open to them. This legislation led to the disappearance of the Catholic middleclass by turning them into peasant farmers. During the 18th century the Protestant ascendancy took total control of Ireland. The ideas of the French Revolution began to percolate into Ireland through Wolfe-Tone, a Protestant Lawyer from Belfast. Tone wanted to unite Irish Protestants and Catholics against restrictive English policies. He founded the 'United Irishmen' and sought aid from the French who sent an expedition to Ireland under General Hoche. This was scattered by a storm in Bantry Bay in 1796. A second expedition in 1798 landed in Killala in Co. Mayo, but after some initial success, the Franco-Irish forces were overcome. Captured, Tone committed suicide. This revolt had heavy consequences for Ireland. On December 15, 1800, the Act of Union was voted in and the Irish Parliament abolished. From then on the country was ruled directly from Westminster.

Discrimination against Catholics continued until the election to Westminster of Daniel O'Connell, a French-educated Catholic lawyer. He began a democratic and pacific campaign which led to the repeal of the penal laws and emancipation for Catholics in 1829, which earned him the title of 'Liberator'.

In the following decades the independence movement continued with the founding of the IRB (Irish Republican Brotherhood) in 1858. A first revolt was stamped out in 1867 and twelve years later the land wars started under the leadership of Charles Stewart Parnell. Parnell, a Protestant landowner elected to the House of Commons in 1875, wanted agrarian reform and home rule, giving Ireland autonomy for internal affairs. Due to an adulterous affair with Kitty O'Shea, Parnell was forced to withdraw from public life in 1890.

The 'home rule' bill was rejected three times by Parliament and in 1892 the Ulster Convention reacted violently against Irish autonomy. Industrialisation of the North drew its largely urbanised Protestant inhabitants into closer links with Britain and guaranteed them access to the vast markets of the British Empire.

Sinn Féin and Partition

The Republican Party 'Sinn Féin' (We Ourselves) was formed in 1905 by Arthur Griffith and immediately demanded the formation of a national parliament. Home rule was finally voted by the British Government in 1912 and signed by the King in 1914, but the outbreak of World War I deferred its application. Profiting from the outbreak of the war, the militant IRB (the future IRA) decided to

Wolfe Tone – Protestant lawyer and founder of the United Irishmen who sought aid from the French against the British forces.

launch an insurrection.

On Easter Monday 1916 they took the General Post Office in Dublin and proclaimed the creation of a provisional government of the Irish Republic. Badly organised, the rebellion failed and its leaders were executed except for the American-born Eamon de Valera, who became president of Sinn Féin in 1917. During elections two years later, Sinn Féin had a landslide victory, but the deputies who refused to sit at Westminster set up an Irish Parliament, Dail Eireann. They also organised the creation of the Irish Republican Army (IRA).

The British Parliament decreed these organisations illegal. Nationalist shootings led to anti-Catholic riots fomented by Protestant Ulster Unionists.

In 1921 after two years of fighting, the Anglo-Irish Treaty led to the partition of Ireland, still rejected by the die-hard IRA republicans. The northern six counties with a Protestant population of one million, and a Catholic nationalist community of 0.6 million, remained loyal to the British Crown.

In the south, the new Irish Free State which was later proclaimed a Republic in 1949, gradually broke away from Britain.

Over three hundred years have passed since the first Tudor planters set foot in Ulster. With civil unrest now part of everyday life, Northern Ireland still remains a victim of its history, its two communities still divided.

Norman Mongan, long-time Paris resident, has just completed a book, "The Menapia Quest", that reveals the long-lost Gallic roots of the Irish – due to be published in 1993.

THE PRESENT

Mark Brennock

The Irish Times Belfast correspondent, Mark Brennock, takes a look at Northern Ireland today and concludes that achieving peace in the province will be a long and painfully slow process.

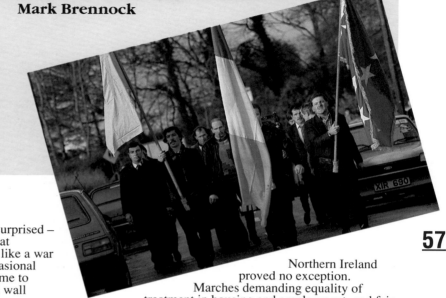

Visitors to Northern Ireland are often surprised – some even vaguely disappointed – that Northern Ireland does not look more like a war zone. You will, of course, meet soldiers at occasional checkpoints, hear helicopters overhead from time to time and read imaginative political graffiti and wall murals in urban working class areas.

But apart from that, you can travel through this often beautiful part of Ireland without being reminded of the conflict at all. The Antrim coast, the Mountains of Mourne, the lakelands of Fermanagh and the lively city of Derry are among the attractive areas that can be visited without seeing much evidence of the conflict. But conflict there is, nevertheless. The death toll since 1969 passed the 3,000 mark in 1992. This is, as optimists point out, a much smaller figure than the number killed in traffic accidents during the same period. But the killings are a manifestation of a tension, bitterness and division that dominates political life and in many areas social life in Northern Ireland.

Since the 1921 treaty that gave independence to what is now the Republic of Ireland, the potential for conflict existed in the six counties that remained part of the United Kingdom.

The Protestant majority dominated not just the parliament at Stormont and the Northern Ireland government, but almost every aspect of life in Northern Ireland.

The large Catholic minority (just under 40 per cent of the population) was excluded from every aspect of public life in Protestant fear that Catholics would subvert the Northern Ireland state if given any power. This is often cited as an excuse for this marginalisation. But the ensuing discrimination in employment, housing, education and politics created deep resentment and discontent among the Catholic population. It was a system that created a potentially explosive situation, just waiting for a catalyst to ignite it. That catalyst was provided by the civil rights movement in 1968 and 1969.

Direct Rule

In the late 1960s, students and others throughout Europe and the US were protesting against perceived injustices in their own countries.

Above: IRA Remembrance Parade. Photo: The Slide File.

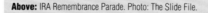

Below: Rosemary Street, Belfast, Photo: Northern Ireland Tourist Board.

Northern Ireland proved no exception.

Marches demanding equality of treatment in housing and employment, and fair voting received widespread support among the Catholic community. These marches and protests were in turn repressed by the physical force of the Stormont controlled police and the local Protestant militia, the B Specials.

The ensuing rioting and violence quickly led to a situation of civil conflict. As the local government failed to control the situation, and the international publicity grew, the British Government acted. They suspended the Stormont Government indefinitely and assumed direct control of the North. The B Specials were disbanded and British troops were sent in.

Initially welcomed into Catholic areas, British soldiers were soon seen by the Catholic population as part of the problem. The notorious incident known as Bloody Sunday, in which 13 unarmed civil rights marchers were shot dead in an afternoon in Derry by British soldiers, sealed the perception in Catholic working class areas that the soldiers were now the enemy.

The Irish Republican Army (IRA), which had become very small and ineffectual over the decades enjoyed a new influx of recruits from the young Catholic population, and a new level of support. British soldiers and police were seen as "legitimate targets" for the IRA, but over the last two decades the IRA's list of legitimate targets has grown ever wider.

Smaller loyalist paramilitary groups, such as the Ulster Defense Association and the Ulster Volunteer Force, have also become semi permanent parts of life in Northern Ireland. They maintain that their killings are in response to IRA actions. The reality is, however, that many of their killings are of uninvolved Catholics, chosen at random. The aim appears to be to strike fear into the Catholic community.

The violence has continued against a backdrop of two decades of failed political initiatives. The British Government has assumed control of almost every aspect of life in Northern Ireland, with local political activity confined to councils that have little power.

With this increased British Government control has come a reduction in many of the original nationalist grievances. Government agencies monitor anti-employment discrimination legislation. Many industries in which employment discrimination was endemic have been forced to change their practices, although the Catholic male unemployment rate is still much higher than the Protestant rate. Discrimination in housing allocation has been all but eliminated. The growth of a prosperous Catholic middle class has been one of the most notable social changes over the last 20 years of direct rule from Britain.

But the British Government's view is that the continuing direct rule is leading to political stagnation. The violence continues at a depressingly steady rate. Local constitutional politicians reject the suggestion that their failure to agree a system of government in Northern Ireland is leaving a political vacuum that is being filled by paramilitary organisations.

The British Government appears determined to fill that political vacuum with some form of agreed local government structure. Statements from British political figures, including Prime Minister Mr. John Major, have suggested that a political settlement reached between the North's constitutional parties, with agreement from both the British and Irish Governments, will isolate the perpetrators of violence and ultimately bring peace. But the political stalemate in Northern Ireland has so far proved immune to political initiatives. The two main unionist parties favour the continuing link with Britain, and oppose any role being given to the Irish Government on the question of government in the North.

The moderate nationalist SDLP, and the political wing of the IRA, Sinn Fein, support a united Ireland, and pursue their aim in different ways. They oppose any "internal solution" that does not give the Dublin government a role in the government of Northern Ireland.

The reasons for the widely differing political aspirations in such a small area can be found in its bloody history, 400 years of which has done little to reduce animosity, particularly in working class areas where support for paramilitary organisations is strongest.

The Anglo-Irish Agreement

At the time of writing yet another political initiative is underway. Representatives of the two main Protestant unionist parties (the Ulster Unionist Party and the Democratic Unionist Party), the middle of the road Alliance Party and the Catholic SDLP are taking part in a complex series of negotiations seeking a new agreement.

Sinn Fein, the political wing of the IRA which wins support of just over ten per cent of the Northern Ireland voters, is excluded because of its support for the

Top: Northern Ireland boasts many areas of outstanding beauty.
Photo: Northern Ireland Tourist Board.I
Bottom: 12th of July Parade – Ulster Orangemen celebrate the victory at The Battle of the Boyne.
Photo: The Slide File

violence of the IRA.

This latest political initiative involves unionist representatives talking to the Irish Government for the first time. But the talks have made little headway, getting bogged down on the long running disagreement of the relationship Northern Ireland should have with the government of the Republic.

Having seen many political initiatives come and go, the people of Northern Ireland do not pin many hopes on such activity, and carry on life as normal without any expectation of a major change in the situation.

Northern Ireland is noticeably more affluent that the Republic, despite the 23 years of violence. It was once the industrial heartland of the island of Ireland, with its shipbuilding, engineering and linen industries making it rival many areas of Britain in terms of industrial development.

The manufacturing industry is now at a very low level, however, and unemployment is the highest in the UK. But the North has been cushioned from the worst of the recession through an annual injection of close to £2 billion from the British exchequer.

Of all regions in Britain and Ireland, Northern Ireland has the highest proportion of its workforce employed by the state. Ironically, the civil conflict has helped create employment in some sectors – such as the police, army, construction and security industries. This helps offset the disincentive for investment in industry that the violence provides.

For the middle classes, life in Northern Ireland is better materially than anywhere else on these islands. Personal taxation is way below the levels in the Republic of Ireland. Property prices in the fashionable areas of South Belfast and the North Down coast are way below equivalent levels in the UK. Middle class people tend to have, as a result, considerably more disposable income than their southern or British counterparts.

Local people have got used to the situation, and in many respects their lifestyle is as normal as it is anywhere else, despite the violence and the constantly visible presence of soldiers and police in the cities.

There has been renewed hope this year for some form of rapprochement between moderate unionist and nationalist politicians. As with every political development in the North progress is still painfully slow. The population has learned not to expect much to happen in a hurry.

A native of Dublin **Mark Brennock** presently resides in Belfast where he works as the Irish Times Northern correspondent.

A PROFILE OF IRISH WRITERS

JONATHAN SWIFT (1667-1745)

Dean of St Patrick's Cathedral in Dublin. Born November 30th 1667 at 7 Hoey's Street, Dublin.

Educated at Kilkenny school and Trinity College, Dublin.

His university career was undistinguished and he obtained his degree only by special exemption. In 1689 he received an appointment as secretary to the statesman, Sir William Temple, at Moor Park in Surrey, England. In 1694, having taken holy orders, he became prebend of Kilroot in Co Antrim but returned to Moor Park in 1696 remaining there until 1699. His duties there included acting as a tutor to the young and beautiful Hester Johnson (Stella) and thus began the great enduring affection of his life.

At Moor Park, he wrote 'A Tale of a Tub' of which he said many years later "What a genius I had when I wrote that book". It was published in 1704, anonymously, like most of his writings. He became Dean of St Patrick's in 1713 and his best known book "Gulliver's Travels" was published in 1726 and became famous almost overnight. The work of his mature and disillusioned years, it reflects in its later parts his savage rage at the spectacle of human misery and depravity. It is one of the great ironies of literature that the voyage to Lilliput became a children's classic.

Swift became increasingly incensed at the ill-treatment of Ireland under English rule. His first pamphlet on Irish affairs, published in 1720, advocated boycotting English fabrics. When Stella died in 1728, Swift was sixty. His remaining years were clouded by infirmity and loneliness. He died on 19th October 1745 and is buried in St Patrick's Cathedral.

OLIVER GOLDSMITH (1728-1774)

Born at Pallas, Co Longford, 10th November 1728. Son of a clergyman. Educated at local schools and Trinity College, Dublin. Having been rejected by the church he went to Edinburgh, to study medicine. He left after two years for Leyden and after having wandered around Europe for two years on foot, he arrived in London penniless but with a dubious medical degree.

He tried various ways of earning a living and then turned to authorship. In 1761 he produced his *Chinese Letters* afterwards published as the *"Citizen of the World"*. The *"Vicar of Wakefield"* (1766) remains a classic of unfeigned charm.

His finest work in verse, *"The Deserted Village"* (1770) with the *"Haunch of Venison"* and the unfinished *"Retaliation"* completes the catalogue of his poetry. Most of his life was passed in poverty and hardship. He died in London of a fever on 4th April 1774.

OSCAR WILDE (1854-1900)

Born on 16th October 1854 at 21 Westland Row, Dublin, he was the youngest son of Sir William Wilde and Jane Francesca Elgee "Speranza". Educated at Portora Royal School, Enniskillen, Co. Fermanagh, Trinity COllege, Dublin, and Magdalen College, Oxford. At Oxford he won the Newdigate prize for poetry in 1878 and acquired a reputation for witty conversation. He graduated with first-class honours in classics and the humanities. In London he became known as the founder of the aesthetic cult and propounded the philosophy of 'art for art's sake'. His first publication was a volume of poems (1881). His real literary career began in 1888 when he published *"The Happy Prince and other Tales"*, a collection of charming fairy stories. His only novel, *"The Picture of Dorian Gray"* (1891) was badly received but his first comedy, *"Lady Windermere's Fan"*, produced in London in 1892, made an instant hit. He followed this success with three more comedies - *"A Woman of No Importance"*, produced in 1893, *"An Ideal Husband"* and *"The Importance of Being Earnest"*, a trivial comedy for serious people, in 1895. His play *"salome"*, written in French and translated into English, was banned in England because it portrayed biblical characters.

"The Importance of Being Earnest" is Wilde's masterpiece, the essence of pure comedy, it has become a classic.

In 1895, Wilde was arrested and charged with homosexual offenses, and on 25th May of the same year, after trial by jury, he was sentenced to two years imprisonment with hard labour. He served the greater part of his sentence in Reading Gaol. In November 1895 he was declared a bankrupt. On his release in May 1897, he left England and spent the rest of his life in Italy and France. In 1898 he published *"The Ballad of Reading Gaol"* based on his prison experiences. In Paris he lived at the Hotel D'Alsasce and on 30th November 1900 he died there of cerebral meningitis after receiving the last rites of the Catholic church. He is buried in the cemetery of Pere Lachaise.

GEORGE BERNARD SHAW (1856-1950)

Born 26th July 1856 at 3 Upper Synge Street, Dublin, now 33 Synge Street, Dublin. He was the orily son of an unsuccessful wholesale merchant and was educated at Wesley College, Dublin. Growing up shy, poor and lonely, Shaw haunted the National Gallery in Merrion Square. At sixteen he went into an estate office as a junior clerk.
In 1872, Mrs Shaw decided to move to London leaving her tippling husband and her shy son to fend for themselves. Four years later young Shaw joined her having made up his mind to become a writer. From 1876-85, Shaw laboured at the writing of five novels, none of which had any success. Having been in and out of various employment, in 1885 he became a book reviewer for the Pall Mall Gazette and as art critic for the world. A year later he became music critic for another

London paper called *"The Star"*. Using the pen name 'Corno di Basseto', the tide had begun to turn as he became known in literary circles. Recognition came when his play *"The Devil's Disciple"* won acclaim in New York and earned more than £2,000 in royalties in 1897. The following year he married Irishwoman Charlotte Payne-Townshend. From then on every year saw a

new play from his pen.
Shaw himself considered *"Heartbreak House"*, produced in New York in 1920, to be his best play. He was awarded the Nobel Prize in 1925 and in 1928 he returned to political writing with *"The Intelligent Woman's Guide to Socialism and Capitalism"* - an example of English prose at it s best.
In 1938 he became ill with pernicious anaemia and after the death of his wife in 1943 the seven remaining years of his life were quiet and solitary. He died on 2nd November 1950. His will benefited the National Gallery of Ireland where as a poor boy he had found the intellectual stimulus for which his heart and mind had craved. The enormous royalties from *"My Fair Lady"*, a film version of *"Pygmalion"*, multiplied the value of this bequest many times over.

WILLIAM BUTLER YEATS (1865-1939)

Born on 13th June 1865 in Sandymount Avenue, Dublin he was the eldest son of John Butler Yeats, a famous Irish painter. Shortly after his birth, the family moved to London and remained there until 1880. He attended school in Hammersmith but spent his holidays in Sligo where his grandparents, the Pollexfens, were millers and small shipowners. He was a delicate and gentle child and was unhappy at school in London. When the family returned to Dublin in 1880, he went to the high school then in Harcourt Street. His father wished him to enter Trinity College as was the family tradition but he refused. Instead, he studied at the Metropolitan School of Art from 1884 to 1885. Here he became friendly with A E Russell and a group of mystics. From seventeen he had been writing poetry and plays and in about 1886 he decided to devote himself to writing, one of his first works being *"The Wanderings of Oisin"*, based on Irish mythology. Then followed *"The Countess Cathleen"* in 1892, his first poetic play. Three books of prose appeared in 1897, *"The Secret Rose"*, *"The Tables of the Law"* and *"The Adoration of the Magi"*.
In 1889 he met the patriot Maud Gonne and his long frustrated obsession with her was one of the great traumatic experiences of his life. He proposed marriage to her in 1891 but was refused. Under her influence he joined the revolutionary Irish Republican Brotherhood and played a prominent part in this organisation. Maud Gonne was the subject of many of his love poems.
Yeats was the creator of the Irish Literary Theatre which had its beginnings in 1899 with the first performance of his poetic play *"The*

Countess Cathleen". In 1902 he wrote *"Cathleen Ni Houlihan"* for Maud Gonne to act in. Yeats later became co-director of the Irish National Theatre with lady Gregory and he became director in 1906 remaining as such until his death.
Some of his most famous works include *"The Wild Swans at Coole"* (1919), *"The Tower"* (1928) and *"The Winding Stair"* (1933).
The insurrection of Easter 1916 made a deep impression on him and he wrote several poems in homage to the executed leaders, one of whom was fellow poet, Patrick Pearse. After the Rising he resolved to live in Ireland full time and he went to live in a small Norman castle in East Galway. With the birth of the new Irish State in 1922, he was appointed to the Senate and in 1923 he was awarded the Nobel Prize for literature. His creative vitality continued into his sixties and seventies. On medical advice, he had spent many winters in Italy and France. Late in the winter of 1938 he left Ireland for the French Riviera in failing health. He died at Roquebrune overlooking Monaco on 28th January 1939. His remains were brought back to Ireland for burial under bare Benbulben's head in north Co Sligo.

JAMES JOYCE (1882-1941)

This poet, novelist and playwright was born at 41 Brighton Square, Dublin on 2nd February 1882, the son of John Stanislau Joyce, an official in the tax office.
He was sent at six years of age to board at

Clongowes Wood Jesuit College but later had to leave this establishment when his father lost his post. He then went to Belvedere College in the northern part of the city and later to University College Dublin where he studied languages. His first published book, an essay on Ibsen, appeared in April 1900. On graduating in 1902, he went to Paris on borrowed money but with neither position or regular income came near to destitution. In 1903, on the death of his mother, he returned to Dublin where he met Oliver St John Gogarty. Joyce failed to find a job and in 1904 after meeting and falling in love with Galway girl, Nora Barnacle, he left with her to live in Zurich.

He later moved to Pola and Trieste where he survived by teaching English in the Berlitz school. He returned to Dublin in 1912 to arrange for the publication of his book of short stories. Disagreement with his publishers thwarted that project and returned to Trieste never to visit Dublin again.

Joyce spent the greater part of the war years from 1914 to 1918 in Zurich. His financial difficulties were relieved by a grant from the Royal Literary Fund and by a number of generous individuals. In 1914 *"Dubliners"* was published, followed in 1916 by *"Portrait of an Artist as a Young Man"*. Encouraged by all of the positive

reaction, Joyce went ahead with his major project, *"Ulysses"*, which was published in Paris in 1922. "Ulysses" brought international fame to Joyce and had great influence on later writers. No work of this century has received so much continuous notice.

In Paris, he worked for 17 years on the book he himself regarded as his magnum opus - *"Finnegan's Wake"*, published in 1939. His remaining works were *"Exiles"*, a play published in 1918, *"Pomes Pennyeach"*, published in Paris in 1927, and an early volume of poems, *"Chamber Music"* (1907).

In 1940 the Joyces moved back to Zurich where the author died on 13th January 1941, and where he is buried.

BRENDAN BEHAN (1923-1964)

Born on 9th February 1923 in Holles Street Hospital, Dublin. He was educated by the Sisters of Charity and the Christian Brothers. He left school at the age of 14 to follow his father's footsteps and become a house painter. In the family tradition, he joined the IRA and was arrested in Liverpool in 1939 for possessing explosives. He was sentenced to three years in Borstal and was released in 1941. He returned to Dublin where he was arrested in April 1942 and condemned to 14 years imprisonment for attempting to kill a policeman. In prison Behan learned Irish from some other internee and he began to write. He was released under a general amnesty in December 1946. He went to live in Kerry and Connemara and spent some time in Paris. In 1954 his first play *"The Quare Fellow"* was produced in Dublin. The play *"The Hostage"* was a runaway success in 1958. The same year saw the appearance of the autobiographical *"Borstal Boy"*. Television appearances and visits to New York, Paris and Berlin for production of "The Quare Fellow" added to Behan's international renown. The warmth and humour of his talk is shown in his later books, *"Brendan Behan's Island"*, *"Behan's New York"* and *"Confessions of an Irish Rebel"*.

Success and money brought their troubles with heavy drinking becoming a problem and, compounded by diabetes, his health finally gave way. He died on 20th March 1964 in Dublin. He is buried in Glasnevin Cemetery.

SAMUEL BECKETT (1906-1989)

Samuel Barclay Beckett was born in Foxrock, South Co Dublin on 13th April 1906, the second son of William Frank Beckett, a quantity surveyor. He was educated at Earlsfort Prep School in Dublin and Portora Royal, Enniskillen, where he achieved excellent academic and sporting records. In 1923 he entered Trinity College where he was placed first in modern literature. Shortly after leaving Trinity he went as an exchange lecturer to Ecole Normale Superieure in Paris where he met James Joyce. In the summer of 1930 Beckett's first work, *"Whoroscope"*

was published in Paris. He returned to Dublin in the same year to take up a position as an assistant lecturer in French at Trinity College but resigned after four terms.

In 1931, *"Le Kid"*, Beckett's first dramatic work, was performed and his first major piece of literary criticism, *"Proust"* was published. Beckett decided to return to live in Paris on a permanent basis in 1932, the same year that saw the publication of *"Wanderjahre"*. The following year his father died leaving him an annuity which formed the bulk of his slender income until the royalties from *"Waiting for Godot"* twenty years later. Beckett continued to write in Paris until 1942 when the Resistance group in which he was active was betrayed to the Gestapo. Beckett escaped to the southern zone of France with only two minutes to spare. Between 1942-45 he helped out as an agricultural labourer during which he wrote his last English novel *"Watt"*. Having returned to Ireland in Easter 1945 to see his family, he readily accepted a post as an interpreter and storekeeper at the Irish Red Cross Hospital in Saint-Lo, Normandy. Back in Paris, Beckett, bursting with creative activity, wrote in French the trilogy of novels, *"Molly Malone Dies"*, *"The Unnameable"* and the play, *"Waiting For Godot"*. "Waiting for Godot" was eventually published in 1952 in Paris and 5th January 1953 saw the world premiere of the same play. The following year Godot was translated into English and the world premiere of the English version was held in London in 1955.

In 1959 his play *"Endgame"* won the Italia prize and four years later at Ulm, West Germany, his drama play was created under the directorship of Deryk Mendel. Beckett won the Nobel Prize for literature in 1969 and he continued thereafter to turn out works of impeccable quality such as *"Breath"*, *"Not I"*, *"Footfalls"*, *"Nacht und Traume"* to name but a few.

He died in Paris in December 1989 where he is buried.

SEAMUS HEANEY (1939-)

Born on 13th April 1939 to Patrick and Margaret Heaney on a farm called Mossbawn near Tamniarn in Co Derry, Northern Ireland. He was the eldest of nine children, two girls and seven boys. His father, in addition to farming the fifty acre Mossbawn, also worked as a cattle dealer. He attended the local school and then went as a boarder to St Columb's college in Derry. He went to Queen's University in Belfast to read English literature and language and graduated with a first class honours degree in 1961. Having left Queens University, Heaney spent one year doing a post graduate teachers training diploma at St

Photo: Peter Zöller

Joseph's, Belfast. During his year at St Joseph's, Heaney did write and he began to read some contemporary works from the Republic.

In 1962 he started to teach in Belfast and the same year saw the publication of his first poem *"Tractors"*. Heaney left schoolteaching in 1963 and returned to St Joseph's as a lecturer in English. He continued to write and to get involved in a literary group which nurtured creative talent. By the time his first collection of poems entitled *"Eleven Poems"* was published in 1965, Heaney's literary career was well underway.

In May 1966 when Heaney was 27, his first full length collection of poems, *"Death of a Naturalist"*, was published. This earned him the prestigious Somerset Maughan

award, the first of amy major literary awards which Heaney has since collected.

As a Catholic from Northern Ireland, Heaney's works have greatly been affected by the troubles of the past twenty years. He was involved in the civil rights movement on behalf of Ulster Catholics which sprung up in the late sixties. Some of his works which have reflections on the Northern situation include *"Preoccupations"* and *"Wintering Out"*. Due to the success of his writings, Heaney left his fulltime lecturer position at Queens University to move to Ashford in Co Wicklow to work as a freelance writer.

By common consent Seamus Heaney is now one of the most important contemporary poets of the English language. He lives in Co Wicklow with his wife Marie and three children.

FROM HARP TO
ELECTRIC GUITAR

Liam McAuley

As the long twilight of an Irish summer shades into darknesss, you enter a pub on the Atlantic seaboard and take a seat at the bar. Like many Irish pubs, it is a place where cultures collide: at one end, in the old-fashioned way, are shelves stacked with groceries; at the back is a gourmet restaurant. In between, under the nicotine-stained ceiling of the main bar, the soft, thick accents of local farmers and fishermen mingle with earnest, enquiring voices from Scandinavia, Germany, France or Italy, hopeful of hearing some Irish music.

Their wish is granted. In due course - for nothing good happens in a hurry - a fiddle and flute strike up a jig or reel that sounds as old as the hills. Soon they are joined by the plaintive notes of a concertina, perhaps also the earthy beat of a "bodhran" (goatskin drum). After a few more dance-tunes, and a slow, sad air, an old man (or just as likely a young girl) is prevailed upon to sing. The song, unaccompanied in the sean-nos style, is highly ornamented, but delivered simply, without any dramatic or dynamic effects; on first hearing, it can sound oddly like the call to prayer of the "muezzin" in a Middle Eastern country.

This is the kind of experience that causes European visitors to Ireland to marvel at the richness and vitality of the country's traditional music, and its ability to bridge the generations. They wonder how it manages to survive and prosper on the threshold of the 21st century. Many of them listen to it with a sense of mingled strangeness and familiarity, regarding it, with both excitement and envy, as a living treasure that has been irretrieveably lost in their own country.

1

1 Music in the streets - a part of everyday life. *Photo: Jole Bortoli*
2 Music in the pubs - listeners and musicians are always welcome.
Photo: Derek Speirs/Report

They are right. For Irish traditional music is the last substantial remnant of a great shared culture with its roots in the feudal societies of the Middle Ages, a culture created over the centuries by the common people of Europe for their own expresssion and enjoyment. This was music the ordinary people could call their own, in contrast to the "art music" of the aristocracy and the Church. It was a music that chronicled and dramatised their everyday world of work, weddings, fairs, markets, love and death. It gave meaning and continuity to their social life and history, which otherwise went largely unrecorded.

Why has the Irish branch of that great European tree continued to grow and sprout new shoots even as the rest has withered? The reason, paradoxically, is that it was cut off - partly by geographical remoteness, but more importantly by centuries of colonisation and repression. Because of this, Ireland did not undergo the vast social upheavals that occurred elsewhere in Europe in the 18th and 19th centuries. The great majority of its people were denied the chance of social advancement, or of any part in the "official" life of the country, and were isolated from social change. So they continued to entertain themselves with the old music, dances, stories and songs and to create new ones within the ancient tradition that was being eroded elsewhere by the new economic and social order. At the same time, the mass emigrations of the 18th and 19th century brought Irish music to the new worlds of America and Australia where its influence is still so marked - in American country and bluegrass music, for example.

When the Normans came to Ireland in the 12th century, their chronicler Giraldus Cambrensis found the native music similar to the music he had heard on the European mainland, except, as he recorded, that Irish harpers were "incomparably more skilled than any nation I have seen. Their style is not, as on the British instruments to which we are accustomed, deliberate and solemn, but quick and lively; nevertheless the sound is smooth and pleasant." The harpers were employed to accompany the poetry declaimed and sung at the courts of the old Gaelic aristocracy and this patronage survived for several more centuries, despite successive waves of Anglo-Norman invaders - many of whom, indeed, became "hibernicis ipsis hiberniores" ("more Irish than the Irish themselves") and took to composing Gaelic poetry in the native style.

But after the great defeat of the Irish at the Battle of Kinsale (1601), which sounded the death knell of Gaelic Ireland, Irish music was outlawed as post-Reformation England set about suppressing what was seen as a rebellious Popish culture. A proclamation of 1603 ordered the extermination of "all manner of bards, harpers, etc" and Queen Elizabeth I herself ordered Lord Barrymore to "hang the harpers wherever found".

In spite of this, harpers survived in dwindling numbers for another two centuries, travelling the roads as mendicant musicians dependent on the charity of their down-trodden fellows, or on the patronage of the new Protestant nobility. Most of their music has been lost, though a number of airs were collected in the late 18th century. The most celebrated of the harper/bards is Turlough O'Carolan (1670-1738), about whom the novelist and playwright Oliver Goldsmith told the following anecdote:

"Being once at the house of a nobleman, where there was a musician present who was eminent in the profession, Carolan immediately challenged him to a trial of skill. To carry the jest forward, his lordship persuaded the musician to accept the challenge, and he accordingly played over on his fiddle the fifth concerto of Vivaldi. Carolan, immediately taking his harp, played over the whole piece after him, without missing a note, though he had never heard it before; which produced some surprise. But their astonishment increased when he assured them he could make a concerto in the same taste himself, which he instantly composed, and that with such spirit and elegance that it may compare (for we have it still) with the finest compositions of Italy".

More than three centuries further on, "O'Carolan's Concerto" is still in the repertoire of musicians such as the Chieftains. While Goldsmith's praise for it may be excessive, it is undoubtedly a piece of great wit and elegance, a kind of Irish-Italian jeu d'esprit.

Even as the old Gaelic nobility and their bards disappeared, the continuing struggle against England during the 17th century led to many contacts between Ireland and Continental Europe, especially France. One result of this was the introduction of new musical forms, instruments and dances. The modern violin, or fiddle, became widespread and the uileann pipes (literally "elbow" pipes) reached their final form through a marriage of the Gaelic warpipes to the French elbow-blown musette. (Unlike the bagpipes, uileann pipes are fed with air from a bag squeezed by the musician's elbow).

Dancing masters toured the country catering for what was clearly, judging by contemporary chronicles, a craze. The English writer Richard Head, observing Sunday pastimes in 1674, saw "in every field a fiddle and the lasses footing it till they are all of a foam". A century later, another observer noted that "dancing is very general among the poor people, almost universal in every cabbin. Dancing masters of their own rank travel through the country from cabbin to cabbin... Weddings are always celebrated with much

3 The Uilleann pipes, a complex and sweet sounding instrument. *Photo: Daniel de Chenu*

4 The Irish harp, one of the oldest traditional instruments. *Photo: Bord Failte*

dancing; and a Sunday rarely passes without a dance."

Many experts are convinced that the 18th century was the period in which Irish traditional music took on most of the characteristics which distinguish it today, and the period in which the bulk of Irish dance music - jigs, reels, hornpipes, polkas, etc - was composed.

The popularity of music and dancing - often, in fine weather, at crossroads, which formed natural meeting places - continued through the 19th century; and at the end of that period the tradition was further strengthened by the revival of interest in the Irish language and culture which accompanied the nationalist movement. At the same time, however, dancing styles became somewhat stylised and regimented by cultural enthusiasts, while crossroads gatherings were suppressed by puritanical clergy alarmed by the drinking and lovemaking they encouraged. But old-style dancing continued to enjoy great popularity up to the 1950s, usually in local parish dance-halls. At such events, music was provided by "ceili bands", in which, because of the need for extra volume and rhythmic drive, the traditional fiddles and flutes were supplemented by accordeons, a piano, and often drums.

After the foundation of the Irish Free State (later the Irish Republic) in 1922, the national broadcasting station, Radio Eireann, devoted much airtime to Irish music; interest was further stimulated by gramophone records by virtuouso performers such as the Sligo-born fiddler Michael Coleman, whose style became greatly imitated.

Though ceili band dancing has waned sharply in the past 30 years, the dance music itself, together with traditional songs and airs, has enjoyed an extraordinary boom. This stems in part from the international 1960s revival of folk music as a reaction against mass-produced electronic culture, a phenomenon that led to the rise of such diverse talents as Bob Dylan, Joan Baez, Tom Paxton, Ewan McColl, and the Incredible String Band. In this climate, the international success of Irish groups such as the Clancy Brothers and the Dubliners gave Irish music a contemporary glamour and encouraged young people to sing and play the old songs and tunes.

Another strong influence was the classically trained Irish composer Séan O'Riada (1931-71), who formed the group Ceoltoiri Cualann to play traditional dance tunes and airs with something of the discipline of a chamber ensemble. By rediscovering old harpers' compositions ("music of the nobles") and by placing the dance tunes on the concert platform, he gave traditional Irish music a new status and respectability and made it fashionable among the urban middle class. At the same time, the music organisation Comhaltas Ceoltoiri Eireann had begun to organise regular "fleadhanna cheoil" (music festivals), which drew huge crowds to different venues around the country.

In time, O'Riada's Ceoltoiri Cualann evolved into the Chieftains, still the pre-eminent Irish music group, and their lead was followed by younger groups such as Planxty, the Bothy Band and De Danann, all in different ways adapting tradtional styles for young, modern audiences. Some well-known Irish rock music performers, such as Van Morrison, Enya and the Hothouse Flowers, have made use of traditional material; some, such as Stockton's Wing and Moving Hearts, have attempted a synthesis of traditional and rock/jazz styles; others, such as Paul Brady and Clannad, have crossed over from traditional to rock; still others, while working in a rock idiom, have acknowledged their debt to a culture in which creating and performing music is a natural part of everyday life - Sinead O'Connor, Chris de Burgh and U2, for example.

Thanks to the revival of the past 30 years, a new generation of young musicians is breathing fresh life into the old tunes so that an ancient tradition manages not just to live, but to grow stronger. Long may it continue!

Liam McAuley is features editor with the Irish Times. He has worked extensively as a journalist in Ireland, Britain and Holland. A native of Belfast he now lives in Dublin.

An international rock star - Bono of U2.
Photo: Eamon Farrell

Photo: National Library of Ireland

EMIGRATION
and The Irish Abroad

by Carol Coulter and Colette Dennison

During the eighties, Ireland experienced the most serious 'brain-drain' the country has ever known as thousands of its young men and women left to seek their future and fortune in such far flung places as Australia, Canada and America.

Those who went were amongst the most-well educated and highly skilled generation that the country produced to date. They emigrated because of the frustration and lack of opportunities created by high taxation and high unemployment (more than 20% of the workforce).

Fired by the world economic recession of the early Eighties, in addition to pressures caused by Ireland having the youngest population in western Europe (almost 50% under 25), university graduates and school leavers saw their future at home as a bleak one - jobless.

Emigration, however, is not a new phenomenon for Ireland or the Irish. Sadly it has always played a major role throughout the history of this country. Despite the 'baby boom' of the past three decades and the subsequent population explosion, Ireland is the only European country whose population today (approx 3.6 million in the Republic) is less than what it was in the mid 19th century (approx 8 million).

One of the major reasons for this lies in the mass emigration sparked off by the Great Famine of 1846-47 which cost some one million lives and changed attitudes to emigration and the pattern set for future generations.

Emigration to the USA and Canada had taken place during the previous century by dissenting Protestants from the north-east. Having had their economic development thwarted by the Anglican Protestant ascendancy, they went voluntarily to the new world to seek their fortune. They left behind a land that was poor and overcrowded. Landlords often favoured emigration as they would have preferred far fewer and more productive tenants.

It was not until the Great Famine however and the total collapse of rent payments that hundreds of thousands of Irishmen and women began to flee and depopulate the countryside. They were convinced that no living could be eked from the land and that the country held no future for them.

Not everyone emigrated voluntarily. Sometimes the land was cleared of people by landlords who wanted it for livestock. People were forcibly deported on coffin ships. Some did not survive the journey to the new world. Others arrived in terrible ill-health. Disgusted by all of this, the then Canadian government officially

Those leaving in search of a new life and possible fortunes chose not only the new world as their destination.

The mills and mines of England and Wales attracted tens of thousands and had the advantage of easier passage money. Some left for the chance to farm land reputedly uninhabited and free in Australia. Political rebels and common criminals were also transported there along with criminals from Britain. Some emigrants left Ireland with a spirit of adventure and wandered off the beaten track ending up in Latin America or Africa. The Chilean national hero, Bernardo O'Higgins, was of Irish

If mass emigration from Ireland has led to the creation of homogeneous Irish communities in the cities of America and Australia, it decimated communities at home. In the worst hit areas of the west coast, the often mentioned beauty of the landscape is matched only by its desolation, as one travels for miles without seeing an inhabited dwelling. Since the last wave of emigration, it is observed that many towns and villages can no longer even field a football team.

Sensing the impact of this over the years, the Irish-Australian writer, Thomas Keneally remarked on "the vacancies and the ghosts" in Ireland.

Illustrated London News courtesy R.T.E.

Others suggest that the heritage of emigration has sapped the energy of the people for change as the young and liberal emigrate leaving an aging population resigned to its lot.

Emigration today is not as final as it was in the 1850's as air travel makes Australia and America more accessible. Many

objected to the British government about the transportation of tenants from Strokestown park House in Co Roscommon.

Emigration however soon became a way of life for the Irish and it continued throughout the century. The historian Gearoid O'Tuathaigh described the situation as follows: "Reluctant parting from home was transformed by the famine into an exodus of mass panic from a stricken land. After the crisis had passed, emigration had become an accepted fact of life in Ireland". This accounts for the fact that although the population numbered 6.6 million in 1851 (after the Famine), it had dropped to 4.4 million by 1911. Today the population of the island as a whole is less than 5 million.

birth and today there are thriving Irish communities in South American countries. As a direct result of all this emigration, some 70 million people living throughout the world now claim Irish origin. Such cities as New York, Boston, London and Liverpool, to name just a few, are bigger "Irish" cities than most cities in Ireland.

Throughout this century Ireland has continued to lose its sons and daughters to other lands. Despite political independence and the promise of economic development that went with it emigration reached a peak in the 1950's before tailing off with the prosperity of the Sixties and Seventies. It rose again to a level of over 40,000 a year in the late Eighties. The destinations were the traditional ones - London, New York, Boston, Sydney.

who emigrated in the Eighties have already begun to return home to raise their families. Those who have chosen to remain in their adopted countries have the possibility of coming back to the 'ould sod' at regular intervals.

Television has internationalised culture, while the growth in ethnic and national identity, world-wide, has made the youth of the Irish diaspora more aware of theirs. Nowadays one finds an interaction between their culture and that of their cousins at home. You can be born in London or Sheffield and be a member of the Irish soccer team or a lead singer with a traditional "Irish" band. Irish emigration is no longer a one way street!

BEING IRISH IN BRITAIN
by Michael Foley

The Irish have done well in Britain. True, those who arrived in the 40's and 50's lived in areas like Camden Town in London (chosen, the legends say, because it was as far as one could walk from Euston station with a cardboard suitcase). They slowly rose up the social rungs however, to be replaced at the bottom by later arrivals from the West Indies. Many left the ghettoes and moved to the suburbs dropping any connection with Irish culture. Assimilation into their adopted culture was speeded up by the fact that they were white and spoke English.

When the Anglo-Normans arrived in Ireland they were said to have become 'more Irish than the Irish themselves'. The process often worked in reverse. Brendan Bracken was an Irishman, born in TIpperary, who rose to become Britain's wartime minister for information and founder of the FInancial Times newspaper. He became so English that he totally denied any Irish background, despite his red hair, and invented a provenance for himself. He claimed he was Australian and he is also believed to have put around the story that he was Winston Churchill's bastard son.

More recently Patrick Cosgrove, a Dublin born journalist, became a leading Thatcherite. He was Mrs Thatcher's biographer and a noted Tory ideologue.

Although a high proportion of young homeless are Irish, many Irish people have done well in a number of professions, notably journalism and broadcasting, as exemplified by Terry Wogan and Henry Kelly. Oddly, they have done less well in politics, despite their strong attachment to the Labour Party and very unlike the Irish in America or Australia.

In total contrast to Irish emigrants in the US and Australia, who have always been very plugged into their roots, the grandchildren of emigrants to Britain have thought of themselves as 100% British.

There has been a huge resurgence of things Irish in recent years with second and third generation Irish now going to learn traditional music and learn the Irish language.

The new emigrant is less likely to want to assimilate into British society totally. He or she is eager to retain a separate identity just as other ethnic groups have done. As that process takes place the Irish in Britain develop greater confidence in terms of their own culture, the culture around them and what they have left behind.

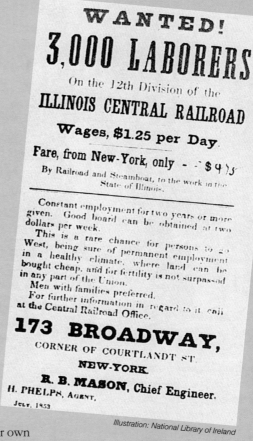

WANTED!
3,000 LABORERS
On the 12th Division of the
ILLINOIS CENTRAL RAILROAD
Wages, $1.25 per Day.
Fare, from New-York, only - - $4ʲⁱ
By Railroad and Steamboat, to the work in the State of Illinois.

Constant employment for two years or more given. Good board can be obtained at two dollars per week.
This is a rare chance for persons to go West, being sure of permanent employment in a healthy climate, where land can be bought cheap, and for fertility is not surpassed in any part of the Union.
Men with families preferred.
For further information in regard to it call at the Central Railroad Office.
173 BROADWAY,
CORNER OF COURTLANDT ST.
NEW-YORK
R. B. MASON, Chief Engineer.
H. PHELPS, AGENT,
JULY, 1853.

Illustration: National Library of Ireland

THE IRISH IN AMERICA
by Harry Brown.

The Irish began to emigrate to the New World in the eighteenth century. Most of them were Protestants from the north of Ireland, descendants of Scottish colonisers. They settled in states like Virginia and Carolina and later day American presidents had this Scots-Irish background.

Many of the so called 'Irish-Americans' of today are descended from Catholic emigrants of the 19th and 20th centuries. Most of these emigrants were tenant farmers and farm labourers driven from the land by poverty, famine and pressure on the inheritance of land. In spite of their rural background, the Irish community in America was and still remains largely urban. For those who came off the notorious 'coffin ships' in the late 1840's, many were unable to go further than Boston or New York due to a combination of ill-health and poverty.

The mid-19th century Irish ghettoes were thoroughly squalid. The Irish with their poverty, their Catholicism and in some cases their own language were despised by the US establishment. Republican party newspapers were inclined to compare the 'dirty, ignorant' Irish unfavourably with slaves and ex-slaves of African descent. But the Irish were needed by a rapidly expanding US economy. By the later part of the century, Irish Catholics were well established in democratic politics, in business, in newspapers and in unions. Their ethnic identity was reinforced by the continual arrival of their compatriots, by

Illustrated London News courtesy R.T.E.

hostility towards new immigrants from southern and eastern Europe and by the ethnic parish structure of the Catholic church in parts of the US.

The flow of emigrants continued after political independence for the twenty six counties slowing dramatically in the 60's and 70's only to reappear in the 80's. Today's "New Irish" reflect the aspirations of modern Ireland. Many are highly skilled and well educated although some still work in traditional Irish occupations: as nannies, in bars, on construction sites. In the Irish communities of cities like New York, Boston, Chicago and San Francisco, they often imbibe the ethnic pride and social conservatism which has come to characterise Irish-Americans.

THE IRISH IN AUSTRALIA
by Carol Coulter.

Irish emigrants to Australia went both voluntarily and against their will, but it was the latter who predominated. These 'emigrants' were transported for both political rebellion and common crime. They were devout Catholics and the Catholic-Protestant divide marked Australian culture and politics deeply.

The transportation of convicts to New South Wales began in 1789 and between 1800 and 1803 a total of eight ships brought 942 Irishmen, a large percentage of whom were United Irishmen or Agrarian offenders. Several leaders of the Young Ireland movement of 1848 were transported there as were the leaders of the Fenians twenty years later. Many escaped from the colony at a later date but have left vivid records of the transportation system.

Because the Irish arrived in Australia at the same time as other immigrants, they were not faced with an established social structure from which they were excluded. They integrated more easily than they had in the United States. Unlike their fellow immigrants to Britain or the USA they did not have the same tendency to congregate in ghettoes.

They were marked off from their new compatriots by their religion. In Australia, "Catholic" became synonymous with "Irish", although a fifth of Irish Australians were Protestants. The Catholic clergy promoted the Irish identity of their flock and the famous Archbishop Daniel Mannix of Melbourne, who ruled from 1917 to 1963, was fiercely nationalist.

The strong identification which most Australians felt with Britain placed the Labour-voting Irish in an oppositionist position. This link with Britain was weakened during the two world wars, and the past few decades have also seen a much more varied immigration into Australia. Today Australians can have Italian or Greek, Chinese or Malaysian names as well as English or Irish names.

In this melting pot a new Australian identity is being forged.

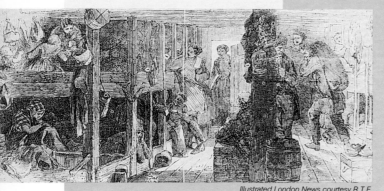

Illustrated London News courtesy R.T.E.

A SORT OF
Homecoming

My adopted Ireland
Tom Kane

I t still seems like yesterday and yet 8 years have passed since I made my first trip to Ireland. Having travelled the world, and even settled for a time in the Far East, the journey itself was of little consequence. Yet I was aware within myself of a curious build up of emotion on arrival at JFK Airport for the flight to Shannon. It was a strange feeling, the anticipation of a journey that was going to be more than a mere opportunity to visit yet another place. This would be a recovery of lost time, a rediscovery of my identity, a sort of homecoming. The feeling crystalized into pure emotion as we broke beneath the early morning clouds above Shannon and I saw, for the first time, the mythical forty shades of green spread before me.

As a second generation New Yorker of Irish descent, I felt that I was completing a journey started 100 years earlier by my grandparents who had left Ireland for the States, like hundreds of thousands of others, during the last century. It was sad to think that neither they nor their children had ever been able to return. Too often this happens in America where only 7% of the population have passports while 20% of the entire North American continent - 50 million people - have one or both parents with Irish lineage.

I've often compared this inertia to the mobility of the Irish. Although many are displaced for economic reasons, their ability to travel the world and be assimilated into other cultures and traditions has given them an influence disproportionate to their relatively small population. At the same time many are returning home, now more globally attuned to business and far better equipped to compete in today's post-entrepreneurial market place. This latent but very significant strength of contemporary Ireland will become increasingly more evident in, and relevant to, the newly emerging Europe. There are not too many countries in the world today where the Irish don't have a foothold and a working relationship within the local economy. Thus for someone from North America looking for business in-roads into the new Europe, Ireland forms the perfect bridge.

My relationship with Ireland took on the nature of a formal "adoption" a few years after my first "homecoming" when I applied for, and received, an Irish passport. I now have dual citizenship - an option granted under Irish law to most second generation Irish, and certainly worth investigating. I thoroughly enjoyed the process of retracing my grandparents' footsteps back to County Galway and indeed to the village of Roundstone. There, the hereditary idiosyncrasies were uncanny! Everyone looked like a relative and when credentials were established, treated me like one. Mannerisms, expressions, the sense of humour, even physical characteristics combined to leave me with a sense of déjà vu, a comfortable, warm feeling of being amongst family again.

Travelling the countryside, the stoic fibre of the Irish becomes self-evident. Ireland's cities may convey a sense of cosmopolitan urban sophistication yet outside of the major cities, where 2/3 of the population lives, it is rural and agricultural. The land has certainly shaped the people, the trials and tribulations of simple farming instilling a fierce but quiet sense of independence and self-reliance - as portrayed magnificently in Noel Pearson's production of John B

Photo: Peter Zöller

Keane's "The Field". The values of home and family are still deeply felt in rural Ireland and most obviously manifest in the quality of the houses - impeccably constructed stone or brick edifices surrounded by solid stone walls, all built to last!

I was most surprised, however, by the quality and consistency of the food produce in Ireland. Although a major exporter of beef, lamb and fish to continental Europe, I'm convinced the Irish keep the best at home. From the Great Irish Breakfast in the morning through to dinner in the evening, be it "haute cuisine" or meat and potatoes, a bad meal is hard to find. There are world-class restaurants in all the major cities as well as scattered throughout the country. Most of the major hotels feature excellent dining facilities.

In 1987 we entered the business world of Ireland with the purchase of a home which later we converted to a hotel. The experience has been a good one in that a number of family members are now deeply

involved in the project at a time in their lives when families begin to scatter. Their Irishness has emerged not only through business but through countrywide friendships that have developed both at home and abroad.

With the deep love of music endemic to the Irish we decided in 1990 to inaugurate a music festival in the west of Ireland, the Adare Festival. Structured as a foundation for the benefit of the arts, it has grown into a major event spread over three week-ends in July with over 16,000 people in attendance in 1991. With a mixture of serious classical music along with more popular acts, it has drawn to Ireland some of the world's greatest performers. In a way I see it as a means of giving back to Ireland something of what the Kane family has received over the last decade.

Tom Kane is a second-generation New Yorker of Irish descent. A business man and patron of the arts, he spends a considerable amount of his time in Ireland.

Island Life

Paul Gosling

The islands of Ireland are ranged along the south and west coasts in a deep and powerful Atlantic.
Their silhouettes are black against a glittering sea or green beneath the chasing clouds. Their stories stretch back beyond the Celts and their peoples have suffered greatly throughout the centuries, witnessing oppression, famine and emigration.
Below, Prof. Paul Gosling of University College Galway writes about these islands detailing their historical past and sketching a picture of how today's islanders have mixed new with traditional in order to survive.

1

Amongst the many fabulous tales of Irish mythology is the wondrous story of Oisin and Tír na nOg, the Land of the Young. This was an enchanted, mist shrouded island, somewhere off the coast of Ireland, in which one stayed forever young amidst perpetual plenty and fair weather. To anyone who has ever sailed out to any of Ireland's 100 or so offshore islands, this picture of island life could not be farther from reality. Yet such themes of island bounty and peacefulness are a persistent feature of Irish literature, past and present. For the 16 island communities which still exist, there obviously remains much affection for, and confidence in, their island homes.

However, the history of Ireland's islands over the the past hundred and fifty years has been one of progressive decline and abandonment. During the fatal population boom of the 18th and early 19th centuries, the number of Ireland's inhabitants peaked at over 8,000,000, many of them living solely off the potato. At this period, the islands of Ireland were teeming places, bristling with whitewashed settlements, tilled fields and bobbing boats. Though picturesque to the detached eye, the populous nature of the islands was no natural thing. Rather, it was the result of a fatal imbalance which forced people out to these sea-girt places because of the scarcity of land onshore. When coupled with a grossly inequitable landholding system which left most of the country, islands included, in the hands of the Anglo-Irish ascendancy, life on an Irish island in the 19th century was, indeed, far from Tír na nOg.

Then came the series of famines, culminating in the horrendous period from 1846-48, when the potato crop failed for three consecutive years, and over 1,000,000 people died as a result. Though the drift from the land had begun before it, the Great Famine opened the flood gates, and so began the steady tide of emigration to England, America and Australia, a silent haemorrhage which to this day remains Ireland's most valuable, and yet, shameful export. From its peak of 399 in 1841, for instance, the population of Tory Island, off the coast of Co Donegal, has gone through an almost unending fall to 335 in 1901, 243 in 1966, 273 in 1971, 200 in 1981 and circa 120 today. On Clare Island, Co Mayo, the fall in population has been even more spectacular, from 1600 in the 1840s, to 690 in 1891, to 168 in 1986.

74

The land reform acts of the late 19th century, and the work of the aptly named Congested Districts Board, did alleviate some of the hardships and lack of facilites for those island communities who remained. However, even with the establishment of Irish independence from Britain in 1922, the decline has continued, and this century has witnessed a host of abandonings: the Blasket Islands, Co Kerry, Inishshark, Co Mayo, Inishbofin, Co Donegal, and the isalnds of Finish and Omey, Co Galway, amongst others. Since the 1960's, the government has however, provided increasing amounts of grant aid to islanders, particularly to those communities within the Gaeltacht, ie, the western parts of Ireland where the Irish language is still spoken. Though well intentioned, this policy has produced its own inequalities and tensions. Thus, while all the islands benefit

from free second level boarding for their children in mainland schools, those in the Gaeltacht get better grants for housing and even more important, for port and ferry facilities.

However, the political tide of neglect is now turning. The genuine interest of Ireland's long serving Prime Minister, Charles J Haughey, TD, in his very own island of Inishvickillane, off the coast of Co Kerry, has, if nothing else, drawn attention to island living. And if the Blasket Islands, off the neighbouring coast of Co Kerry have been abandoned since the 1950s, they have bequeathed to us the vivid literature of Peig Sayers and Tomas O'Crohan. Other Irish writers have either hailed, or drawn inspiration, from islands, particularly those of Co Galway. Liam O'Flaherty and Sean O'Riordain both hail from the Aran Islands, where in the glow of the Irish Literary Revival at the turn of the century, such notable figures as W B Yeats and J M Synge found inspiration in the daily toil and stories of the islanders. Further north lie Inishbofin and Clare Island, whose daunting landscapes have inspired both poets and academics, most notably Richard Murphy and Robert Lloyd Praeger. The latter's unrivalled interdisiplinary study of Clare Island, published by the Royal Irish Academy between 1911 and 1915, provided a model for all subsequent island researchers.

1-2 Atlantic storm - Atlantic tranquility. *Photos: Bill Doyle*
3 Traditional mode of transport to the islands, the currach, light and manouverable. *Photo: Bill Doyle*
4 Old island couple at prayer. *Photo: Bill Doyle*
5 Currach amongst the dry stone walls, Aran Islands. *Photo: Bill Doyle*

Yet despite their problems, the 16 island communities which still survive are far from gloomy or despairing. Being naturally optimistic and stoical, the visitor will find in them a people of generous spirit, teasing humour, and keen intellect. Ready, at the drop of a hat, to abandon the job in hand and engage you in conversation about a bewildering range of topics: life in the cities, the price of sheep, space travel, or the EC. Indeed, you can often find yourself drawn into mildly embarrassing conversations concerning a neighbour's bad habits or meanness. Such preoccupations are undoubtedly the result of the isolation of the winter months. However, with the heady days of summer come the lambs and tourists, the skidding clouds and soaring seabirds, to lift the spirit, lighten the eye, and revitalize the blood.

Economically, the income of islanders is generally diverse, being often based on a combination of sources: some fishing, a flock of sheep, and the "dole" or **government benefit** to small farmers. And depending on the family, perhaps the "American Letter", the famous envelope from a brother or father abroad, bringing not only tidings from another world but also a welcome cheque or parcel of bright clothes for the young ones. Though traditional livelihoods such as fishing are still important contributors to the family's purse, the back breaking jobs of drawing the seaweed from the shore to fertilize the fields, or burning the rods of kelp to extract the iodine, are now thankfully things of the past.

Though each community is unique in its own way, the visitor to more than one island may soon discern a recurrent social pyramid with its attendant representatives: the chatty, man of the world, hotelier or guest-house owner; the grumpy by day but effusive by night, publican; the polite curate; the proudy island nurse; the fretful grocer; the good-time, bar-stool boyo, the brooding batchelor farmer. Each is quite different from the next, but somehow the same, as if each member of these small, tight-knit communities is genetically fated to fulfil a necessary role. Soon too, you will discern the healthy disrespect of the islanders for their rusting cars, motorbikes and vans, on which one rarely sees the obligatory insurance disk or even proper registration plates!

And what would you do for a day, not to mention a week, on an Irish island? Well, the choice is as broad as your mind. There is the shared enjoyment of the summer schools, such as those organized annually on Inishbofin, Co Galway, or Clare Island, Co Mayo. Or if you seek tranquility there are endless walks on the panoramic hills and shining cliffs of Tory Island or Aranmore, in Co Donegal. Rain gear is essential though, given the rainbow of weathers one can encounter, ranging from moist, to misty to windy or blue skied. Then there is the frequent opiton of boat trips to a neighbouring island, or for a day's fishing on the swaying sea. And for those resistant to its refreshing temperatures, try snorkelling or scuba diving in the

vivid, clear offshore waters. What about a visit to the rich local antiquities of Inisheer, or to its newly arrived offshore fish-farm. And at the end of the day, wholesome, sea-fresh food, followed by a bedtime book or a stroll to the pub. But beware the hours of entertainment which, given the rarity of island policemen, will often not commence until 11pm or so. Fueled by animated conversation, alcohol and a Ceili such gatherings often run well into the small hours.

Amidst the human heartbeats, there are also abundant remains of previous island worlds. The tombs of Neolithic farmers, for example, are a feature of the rich archaeological remains of the Aran Islands. And on Inishmore, the largest of these three stark protrusions of bare limestone, is Dun Aonghasa. This massive cliff-top fort is one of the most spectactular prehistoric monuments in Western Europe. For reasons that we cannot fully comprehend, the early generations of Irish Christian monks were particularly attracted to the islands off the west coast. What, but God, could have lured the nameless community of monks out on to the bare and dizzy heights of Skellig Michil, off Co Kerrry, to build corbelled stone beehive cells in the 7th or 8th century AD. Though also long abandoned, the well preserved monastic ruins of Inishmurray, Co Sligo, indicate a more settled and propserous religious community from the same period. Picturesque early church ruins are, in fact, a frequent sight on the islands of Galway and Mayo, but of them all, Inishmore in the Aran Islands contains by far the most numerous and best preserved examples of ecclesiastical remains.

For the naturalist too, there is also abundant opportunity for viewing the numerous species of seabirds, along with dolphins, seals and even whales. The uninhabited Saltee Islands, off the south coast, offer facilites for the serious ornithologist to view its myriad communities of migratory seabirds. In fact, this small island is one of the most important stations in Europe for studying their life cycles.

Today, some of the western islands are facing a new threat, potentially even more fatal than emigration - the spectre of gold fever. The discovery of commercially viable gold bearing rocks on Inis Turk, in Co Mayo, recently prompted the islanders there to threaten a total blockade against the prospecting engineers and the mining moguls. Their fear is that the processes involved in extracting the gold will actually consume a large part of this 'Island of the Wild Boar". In fact, it is in their simple unspoilt character that the richest assets of

Photo: Bill Doyle

Ireland probably lie. Tourism, though it is undoubtedly an undermining influence on the Irish language on the Gaeltacht islands, is beginning to quietly supplement the income of many families, whether in the form of a cosy guesthouse, a co-operative display centre and knitwear shop, like that on Inishmaan, or the fine pottery workshop on Cape Clear Island, off the coast of Co Cork. Such ventures are beginning to provide much needed jobs for the islanders, facilities for the visitor, and hopes for a brighter island future.

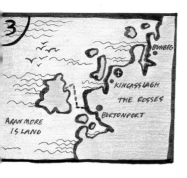
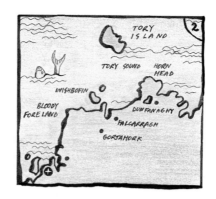
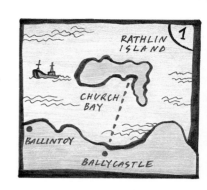

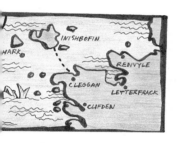

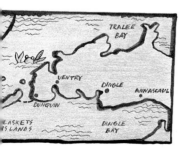
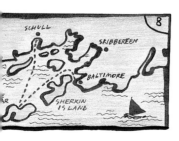
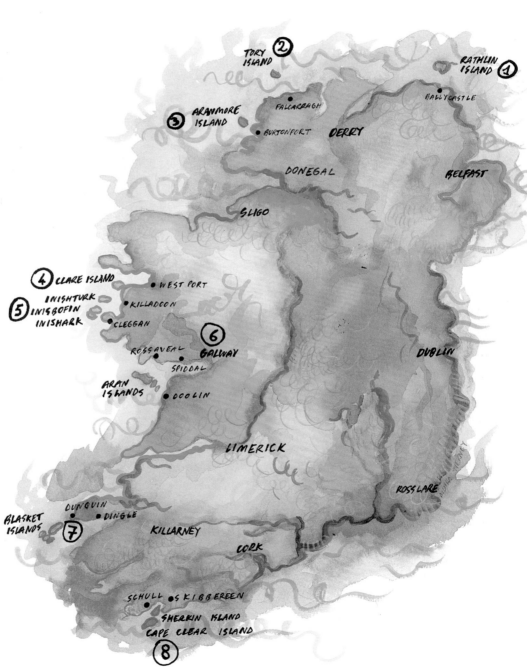

A Day in the Life of an Islander

Morning. A Thursday in October. An overcast dawn after a night of wind and rain. The islanders rise late and early, according to habit.

Within signs of a clearance from the south-west, men can be seen making their solitary way towards the piers, to check the boats at their moorings, or to the hill, to check the sheep. Word is out that the vet may get in to the island today from the mainland; she's waited in vain at the mainland pier three times over the last few days but the island mail boat couldn't tie up; sure even a whisper of a swell at that damn pier and your boat would be smashed to pieces in no time.

From the scattered houses, the chimney smoke bends skywards. The time worn division of labour is still strong, as the women tend to their washing and preparing the dinner - the main meal of the day is at 1pm or perhaps 2.30pm when the children come home from the school. There's only 28 of them now since the Caseys left for the mainland last year.

As the children struggle homewards, their heads turn toward the hammering, as the roofing felt is tacked on to the new house in Middlequarter: the first house to be built on the island for 20 years or more. Say what you like about it, but the fish farm is jobs and jobs mean the young people will stay on the island.

Thursday. That means the pub will be open tonight and the card-school's on again. The weekend is coming, and with it, weather permitting, will come the daughter working in Dublin or perhaps some of the teenagers home from boarding school.

By 4pm the light is fading and the windows begin to light up, calling the family home for tea. Fetch turf for the fire. Maybe the curate will call - he's good crack.

Night follows quickly on the tails of a magnificent russet sunset, its beauty tainted in the islanders' eyes by the fore-knowledge of the long winter ahead.

Photos: Daniel de Chenu

TRAVELLING TO THE ISLANDS

"Islands of Ireland", produced by the Irish Tourist Board, is an excellent colour fold-out brochure giving details of Ireland's principal inhabited and uninhabited offshore islands. It contains a lot of practical information on travel arrangements, accommodation and the facilites available on each island. Published by Bord Failte, the Irish Tourist Board, price IR £1.50. Available in all Tourist Information Offices, in English, French and German editions.

FURTHER INFORMATION

Guide books and/or maps for the visitor, are now available for many of the inhabited islands. As yet, however, these are invariably in English language versions only. Amongst them, Tim Robinson's "Oileain Arainn", a map and guide (Folding Landscapes, 1980, price IR £ 3.44), and his lyrical "Stones of Aran" (Penguin, IR £6.90), are particularly noteworthy.

Perhaps the finest piece of writing to have ever emerged from an Irish island is Tomas O Crohan's, "An tOileanach", The Islander. This moving autobiography of a Blasket islander is a notable contribution to European literature, and is available in an English translation (Oxford University Press, IR £5.50).

Paul Gosling is professor of archaeology at University College Galway. He has travelled and researched extensively on many of the islands off the west coast of Ireland..

DINGLE
HISTORY AND NATURE

Steve MacDonagh

1

Nor is the most remarkable quality of the place its extraordinary heritage in stone monuments. Here Iron Age promontary forts defend the craggy coastline and menhirs stand in mute testimony to earlier inhabitants. A series of inscribed stones suggests that an early form of writing called *ogham* originated amongst the people of this area. On a narrow strip of hillside poised precariously above cliffs are the remains of hundreds of stone huts shaped like beehives. Sixty small settlements of the early pioneers of Christianity are strung like rosary beads along the route of an old pilgrimage road.

The special quality of the penninsula - the Dingle experience - is much less easy to define and describe than beehive huts and rock formations, but it has to do with the position of Dingle at the far western periphery

The most remarkable quality of the Dingle Penninsula is not its scenery, even though the National Geographic Traveller has described it as "the most beautiful place on earth".Thrusting out into the Atlantic Ocean and almost entirely surrounded by water, the mountainous land meets the sea in dramatic coastal rock formations and long, sweeping, golden strands. The light provides an inexhaustable attraction for artists and ordinary mortals alike; looking out over the vast expanse of the ocean one can see the light change within half an hour from delicate yellow, azure, pink and white to lowering dark purple gashed with gold and vermillion as clouds march in from the western horizon like some massive army of the gods.

of Europe, where it has remained untouched by an industrisal revolution and has retained too a stubbornly regional character, almost immune from the contagion of central political power. Yet, for all

its apparent isolation it has both an international past and a cosmopolitan present.

Quite easily accessible, even in prehistoric times by sea from both Scandinavia and the Mediterranean, these coasts were settled in the Bronze Age by iron workers who manufactured and exported prestige weapons from here. Later, Vikings exported butter and hides from the harbour of Smerwick; the same harbour was in the 13th century taken over by Florentine merchants, and in 1580 a joint Papal and Spanish force of six hundred soldiers was masacred there by the English army. Dingle harbour became the primary port of the area and enjoyed substantial trade with Spain. Prevented by English conquest from playing leading roles in their own society, the sons of leading families contributed to the military, religious, cultural and commercial establishments of many European countries. One Dingle man, an officer of the Irish brigade in France, prepared a house in his home town for Marie Antoinette as part of a plan to rescue her from the guillotine.

There were other ways in which the Dingle Penninsula was less isolated from continental Europe than might appear. In medieval Europe one of the most frequently copied manuscripts was the Navigatio of Saint Brendan, an account of his voyage from Brandon Creek on the Dingle Penninsula to the "Heavenly Isles". And in Historia Naturas, published in 1635, John Eusabius Nieramberg referred to the reputation, widely known throughout Europe, of the Dingle Penninsula as an extraordinary nature reserve with an abundance of wildlife which he ascribed to the sanctity of the early Christians who had established their modest settlements in such numbers here. Throughout Europe it was known by the nobility as one of the best sources of falcons, particularily peregrine falcons.

The combination of determinedly local characteristics with international influences continues to the present day. The living heritage of language, custom and song contribute enormously to the feeling that Dingle is a very special place. But this heritage, although specific and local, is not inward looking and inaccessible. The Irish language, which is still spoken here, is one of the most ancient in Europe and in it a special world view and way of being are expressed. Also, customs which died out long ago elsewhere in Europe were maintained here in Dingle within living memory, and some still are. Irish traditional music flourishes as a living thing, with none of the "quaintness" of folk revival, and has in recent years attracted many musicians and admirers from other countries.

1 Sunset over the Blasket Islands, Dingle Penninsula, Co Kerry. *Photo: Peter Zöller*
2 Hiberno - Romanesque church and stone cross, Kilmalkedar, Dingle. *Photo: Peter Zöller*

The customs that strike the visitor are the small ones, the mannerisms. Dingle people as they pass in the street always greet each other with a gesture and a word or two. As you stand at the bar in a pub or sit at a table in a cafe you may find that a Dingle person is asking you where you are from, remarking on the weather and engaging you in a discussion about anything under the sun. For there is almost nothing Dingle people cannot converse about, and they can weave stories from the simplest of elements.

The essence of the Dingle experience and of the Dingle character is a special kind of relaxed, unhurried spontaneity. This can be infuriating if you urgently need directness and speed, but the secret in Dingle is to slow down and take it easy. Visitors enquiring about the time, place and cover charge for a traditional music "session" in a pub may be confused to find that the publican doesn't seem very sure. The fact is that the best sessions take place when the musicians happen to be feeling in the mood, and there is no cover charge. Informality is general and many of the best pubs seem like the extended front rooms of private houses. The true traditional music session is not something you can book for like La Scala or for a Shakespeare play at Stratford in England, or even going to a baseball game in the USA. It is woven into the fabric of everyday life, and is more or less taken for granted.

3

3 Main Street, Dingle. *Photo: Peter Zöller*
4 Dingle harbour, a lively fishing port. *Photo: Peter Zöller*
5 Gallarus Oratory, Dingle Penninsula. *Photo: Peter Zöller*

So when in Dingle, change down a gear or two. Relax, give yourself time to look around you and to listen, and take the way of life here on its own terms. For many people habituated to the demands of city life there can be no more healing and renewing experience in the world.

DINGLE TOWN

For most of the year this is the best place around which to let your stay revolve, but in July and August it can be too crowded for some tastes, in which case quieter parts of the peninsula are only a few minutes' drive away. The visitor concerned to wake up to a beautiful view may be best advised to stay outside the town - a few miles west in Ballyferriter, or a few miles north on Tralee or Brandon Bays - but for the convenience of being able to enjoy a wide choice of pubs, shops and restaurants, there can be no better option than to stay in Dingle. Also, it is a pleasant little fishing town in which almost every house is painted a different colour; its harbour has recently been improved, and from the pier one can take a short trip in a small boat to see a famous and delightful dolphin which lives at the mouth of the harbour.

EATING AND DRINKING

The peninsula is excellently provided with restaurants, most of which specialise in seafood, and with pubs, many of which feature traditional music. There are more than twenty restaurants in Dingle town and the variety is considerable, but almost all specialise in seafood, which is guaranteed to be absolutely fresh. A few of the restaurants have interesting wine lists, but Irish people are not great wine drinkers, preferring for the most part the distinctive Irish beer, Guinness. There are also a few restaurants in the west and in the north of the peninsula. All of the pubs serve Guinness, but apart from that they can

vary greatly. One in Dingle is a leather shop which sells boots and shoes as well as being a pub; another is a hardware store - on one side the bar, on the other side kettles, fertiliser, string, clocks... a seemingly chaotic collection of goods. The secret to enjoying the pub culture of the peninsula is to sample as many pubs as you can and, when you find one you really like, stay there! For reasons of safety this delightful exercise is best carried out in Dingle town where one can walk from pub to pub.

ACCOMMODATION

There are three hotels in Dingle town: Benners (situated in the heart of the town; old-fashioned in style though completely rebuilt in 1983), the Skellig (modern, beautifully sited, with swimming pool and sauna) and the Hillgrove (most noted as an entertainment hall featuring music and dancing, but also providing accommodation). There are also hotels in Ballyferriter: Granville's (old-fashioned, informal) and the Dun an Oir (modern, with golf course and chalets); and Castlegregory: Crutch's (old-fashioned, in pleasant wooded setting) and the Tralee Bay. Many visitors find it a particular pleasure to enjoy the intimate ambience of be and breakfast guesthouses and farmhouses, of which there are many all over the peninsula. A list of all kinds of approved accommodation is available at the tourist office Dingle.

GETTING AROUND

The roads offer spectacular viewsSlea

Itineraries

Fourteen detailed touring itineraries specially compiled for The Ireland Series by some of Ireland's most experienced tour guides.

DUBLIN - CLONMACNOISE - GALWAY

"Through the heartland of Ireland, across its beautiful green and rolling countryside, through its attractive small country towns, with a visit to one of the country's most important monastic sites at Clonmacnois before arriving in Galway – capital of the West."

Leave **Dublin** via the **N4**, the main road to the west of Ireland. Cross the river *Liffey* at **Leixlip** at which point we enter the county of *Kildare*. This county is perhaps best noted for its many stud farms, some of which we will see en route. Continue on the main road towards **Maynooth**, with its wide main street, an indication that was once a manorial village serving *Carton House* (behind walled estate on our right before entering Maynooth) an 18th century former residence of the *Earls of Kildare*.

Continuing to the end of the main street we see the entrance to *St. Patrick's College*, an important catholic ecclesiastic centre, a seminary for training priests and also a university.

Leaving Maynooth we travel towards **Kilcock** with the *Royal Canal* on our left (one of the two canals that flow into Dublin). We follow the main road to **Kinnegad** where we join the **N6** for Galway. This route takes us past a series of small attractive villages and rolling

Clonmacnoise

green countryside. The first village is **Rochfortbridge** named after *Robert Rochford*, a 17th century member of Parliament and friend of *Jonathan Swift*. Further on we come to **Tyrrellspass**, one of the prettiest villages in *Westmeath* which once

was a national tidy town winner. It received its name from the Anglo-Norman Tyrrell family who ruled here up to Cromwellian times. A 15th century castle still stands at the end of the village and is now a private residence. This very attractive village was laid out in its crescent form by *Lady Belvedere* in the 18th century.

Travelling on we arrive at **Kilbeggan** on the river *Brosna* noted mainly for the presence of an old *whiskey distillery* which is now an industrial museum and craft centre.

Further en route we stop at **Horseleap** which got its unusual name following the leap by the Norman *baron de Lacy* over the castle drawbridge while being pursued by some native chieftains. Soon after we arrive at Moate a village which was founded by Quakers in the 17th century.

Beside the still inhabited castle lies a *Quaker cemetery*. **Moate** lies in the centre of a very rich cattle raising area and has a large cattle mart and milk pasteurising plant.

About 9km beyond Moate we leave the main route to **Athlone** to travel to **Clonmacnois** on the **N62**. Clonmacnois, which translates as the meadow of the son of Nois, is one of the country's most impressive monastic sites. Although mainly in ruin, the site boasts interesting round towers, many small churches, a cathedral and three high crosses.

Leaving the splendours of Clonmacnois, we follow the river *Shannon* to **Shannonbridge**. Here we have a choice to travel to **Birr** on the **R439** and see its famous *castle* or continue along the **R357** to **Ballinasloe** in Co. Galway. **Ballinasloe** on the river *Suck* is renowned for its October *horse fair*, the largest in Ireland. This busy commercial centre is also one of the most important in the bloodstock industry.

Leaving the town we travel along the main road to **Galway (N6)** about 8 km out of Ballinasloe we notice the signs indicating the *Battle of Aughrim* (the village lies near the main road). This battle took place in 1691 and led to the defeat of the catholic Irish and French forces by *William of Orange's* soldiers and was a major battle in Irish history.

We continue on and pass through the busy little town of **Loughrea**. The cathedral here contains some of the finest stained glass windows in the whole of the island. The 20th century artists involved were *Michael Healy, A.E. Childe and Evie Hone*. From Loughrea we travel onto the city of **Galway**, the gateway to *Connemara*.

Total distance: 243 km.
Public transport: 7 day week service between Dublin and Galway. Contact Bus Eireann 01-366111

THE BEARA PENINSULA

"From rock strewn desolation to wooded glens and luxuriant gardens warmed by the Gulf Stream: the coastline of the Beara Peninsula twists 'round creeks, sandy bays, harbours and headlands, luring the traveller to fresh discoveries."

From **Glengarriff** at the head of *Bantry Bay* we set off due west along the **R572** to discover the splendours of the Beara Peninsula. Beyond to our right rise the mountains of *Caha* and the *Glen of Coomarkane* with its mighty glacier-cut corrie lakes at its head. The rocks of the mountains themselves are all rounded and smoothed by the passage of the ice sheets, which carried and then, on melting, dropped many big boulders which now perch as erratics here and there on the hills. These hills are well worth climbing, but though they rise just over 600m, remember that the Irish weather can change very rapidly and conditions can be very severe on these heights.

At **Adrigole** look up to *Hungry Hill*, 687 m, a very attractive mountain. Set half way up its rocky face is a rocky shelf on which are two corrie lakes – they feed a 214m cascade to the Adrigole valley, a very fine sight after rain. From the village of Adrigole, a fine mountain road climbs over the **Healy Pass** to Lauragh on the other side of the peninsula and Co. Kerry.

Our tour continues directly to **Castletownbere** a fishing port and good centre from where to explore Beara. Its bay, sheltered by *Bere Island*, was once a British naval base. The island today is a sailing school base.

Castletownbere has a group of boulder burials on the hillside near the old waterworks, and a fine stone circle on its western side. Here too, are the remains of the old castle and star shaped fort of *Dunboy*, where an Irish and a Spanish force stood siege in 1602 by the English forces under *Sir George Carew*, and were finally overwhelmed. The old fort has been excavated and can be explored easily.

From **Castletownbere** the road leads on right to the end of the Beara Peninsula and the narrow sound with its violent tidal race between the mainland and **Dursey Island**. Access to the island is by cable car – the only

Allihies

cable car in Ireland. *Dursey* is a beautiful long mountain island, rimmed by high cliffs with an old signal tower on its heights and wide views all around to, among other things, the cow, calf and bull rocks.
From *Dursey* we follow the northern side of the peninsula to **Allihies**. This was the site of extensive copper mines which opened in 1812. The 19th century was the main period of prosperity and Cornish workers who were brought in as the technical experts were housed in their own *'Cornish village'* of which some ruins survive. Some working and exploration of the mines continued until 1962. Nowadays old engine houses stand in picturesque ruin of the scarred hillsides. from **Allihies** we continue to **Eyeries**, a small village set back from the sea on a pleasant bay.
A little east of it is the tallest ogham-inscribed pillar stone in Ireland, at **Ballycrovane**. It is over 5.18m high; the inscription reads: MAQI DECCEDDAS AVI TURANIAS (to the son of Decceddas, nephew of Turanias).
There are many other standing stones and boulders in this district; another fine stone circle at **Ardgroom** and yet another at the head of the valley that runs up into the hills from **Lauragh**.
Beyond Ardgroom we cross into Kerry. The road now follows the line of the *Kenmare "river"*, another drowned valley, to **Kenmare**. On the way we pass a beautiful valley running back into the hills with lakes on its floor *(Clonee and Inchiquin lakes)* and a higher circle of corrie lakes under the peaks above. At the head of this valley is a fine waterfall. The return to **Glengarriff** from **Kenmare** is made by the **tunnels** road, a fine mountain highway which climbs up to cross the ridge along which the county boundary runs, by means of a long tunnel. On both sides the road commands some spectacular panoramic views over *Kerry and Cork*.

Total distance: 136 km approx.
Public transport: not available

DONEGAL – THE INISHOWEN PENINSULA

'Past ancient sites and sensuous scenery to the Republic of Ireland's northernmost point.'

Leaving **Downings** and returning to **Carrigart** we travel along *Mulroy Bay* to **Milford** and **Ramelton**.
Ramelton, a planter's town was begun in the early 17th century and has a lot of character. Continuing along the Western shore of *Lough Swilly* we arrive at **Letterkenny**, the most populous town in the county.
To reach the *Inishowen Peninsula* we take the western road from Letterkenny to **Buncrana**, namely the **N13**.
Our first stop is **Manorhamilton** on the east of the river *Swilly estuary* with the *Doorish Mountains* rising to the East.
From here we make our way northwards for approx. 8 km before turning off for a 2 km uphill drive to the *Grianan of Aileach*.
Here on top of *Grianan Mountain* (250 m) is a stone fort enclosed within three earthen banks, the site of a tumulus and of an ancient approach road. What dominates is the reconstructed (1870s) stone fort. The diameter of the cashel is over 23 m. The interior of the wall is stepped in three terraces with four flights of steps. There are two pasages within the wall, one from the south and one from the northeast. The place has been used for a long time and the earthen enclosures date from the iron age when it was used as a temple of the sun. The stone fort is much later and dates from historical times. *Ptolemy of Alexandria* noted its position in the 2nd century A.D. Exquisite views of the surrounding countryside are offered to the naked eye from atop the walls.
From the Grianan we return to the N13 and continue to **Fahan** where we find a few traces remaining of *St. Muran's Abbey*. The most interesting item is a flat two-faced cross. Archeologists have deciphered the writing on the north face. It is a Greek version of the Gloria Patria dating from the mid-7th century.
Travelling along the eastern shore of Lough Swilly from Fahan we arrive at **Buncrana**, a seaside resort and excellent shopping centre. There is a fine beach at nearby **Lisfannon**. The road north climbs through beautiful vistas of sea and mountainside to the *Gap of Manore*. At the summit breathtaking views of the *Lough Swilly* area and the Atlantic beyond are offered. We descend to **Clonmany** to view the waterfall nearby at **Glenview**. A little further on is the delightful village of **Ballyliffen** with a fine sandy beach at **Pollan**.
Veering due east at Ballyliffen we travel to **Carndonagh**, an important ecclesiastical site dating from the 5th century.
Its 1945 catholic church is a good example of modern church architecture in Ireland. Less than one kilometre away we find *St. Patrick's Cross*, which expert opinion holds to be the

oldest standing cross in Ireland. It is by the roadside opposite the protestant church and is one of the most important examples of early Christian crosses outside mainland Europe. Leaving Carndonagh we go through comparatively good land to reach the village of **Malin** (17th C.), the most northerly settlement in the Irish Republic. On the nearby *Hill of Dean* is a well preserved monument called the *Temple of Dean*.
13 km further on we reach *Malin Head* where we find an early 19th century signal tower and a ship's radio station which is still in use. Spectacular seascapes are offered from the Malin Head looking out to the wild Atlantic ocean.
The 'wee' house of Malin is a rock cell cut into the cliff. It may have been an anchorites cell. Returning via the coast to **Culdaff** we spot several fine sandy beaches which are safe for bathing. Three km south of **Clonca** is the impressive shaft of *St. Boden's cross* rising to a height of 4 m.
Close by we find ruins of a 17th century planter's church and further on between Culdaff and Moville we can see an example of an ancient sweathouse with a circumference of 12 m.
Moville on Lough Foyle was once a port of call for trans-atlantic liners but has found a new role as a leisure centre.
The drive between Moville and **Muff** takes us along the western shore of Lough Foyle looking onto **Derry** and *Northern Ireland*. From Muff, a small border village, we make our way back to **Letterkenny** via **Newtown Cunningham** and **Manorcunningham**.

Total distance: 250 km.

Public transport: Regular bus services between Letterkenny and Buncrana This trip is not easily made by public transport.
Contact: Bus Eireann at Ramelton Rd., Letterkenny.

83

Grianan of Aileach

DUBLIN - KILKENNY

"*From Dublin's magnificent soutern coastline through the wooded hills of Wicklow. Visit the splendor of the Powerscourt Gardens and the historic monastic site of Glendalough. View the prehistoric Browneshill Dolmen in Carlow and explore the medieval city of Kilkenny*".

84

Leave Dublin via the **Merrion Road** and continue along the coast road to **Dun Laoghaire,** a major ferry port and yachting centre. A stroll on the pier beyond the yacht clubs is most refreshing.
Continuing along the coast towards **Sandycove** where the small round *Martello Tower* houses the **James Joyce Museum** we turn onto the *Sandycove Road* and head for **Dalkey** Village. Drive along the coast on *Coliemore Road* where we have an excellent view of *Dalkey Island.* Continue along the *Vico Road* with the superb view of *Killiney Bay* and Dalkey and Killiney hills on our right. Driving southwards towards **Bray** we turn right before Bray and follow the signposts for the picturesque village of **Enniskerry**. On the

Glendalough

outskirts of Enniskerry lie the magnificently laid out **Powerscourt Gardens**, developed over 30 years in the 19th century in the grand Italian style. They contain a fine collection of statuary, balustrades and fountains and are noted for their extensive collection of conifers

from all over the world. There is a fine view of the *Sugarloaf Mountain* in the distance.
Leaving the estate we take the road southwards heading for **Roundwood**, a small village dominated by the large reservoir which serves Dublin.
From Roundwood fork right for **Glendalough.** En route to the monastic site we enjoy a pleasant trip over the peaceful hills and bogland dotted with sheep and the many small farmholdings so characteristic of Co. Wicklow.
At the junction in **Laragh** we follow the road to the right for **Glendalough**. On our left hand side along this road we have a view of some of the dispersed ruins of the monastic site. Continueing on straight beyond a fork in the road we turn left into the carpark of the *Glendalough Visitor Centre.*
In the visitor centre we can see the exhibition on the monastic life in early Christian Ireland and a short audio visual show on early monastic Ireland, followed by a guided tour of the monastic site. Glendalough contains a splendid round tower almost 1000 years old as well as the tiny oratory popularly known as *Saint Kevin's Kitchen* (due to it's chimney-like belfry) , the plain granite cross known as *Saint Kevins Cross,* and other important

ruins. Enjoy a picnic just outside the monastery grounds or have lunch in the hotel or cafe nearby. Also enjoyable is a 15 minute walk to the nearest of the two lakes which gave Glendalough its name (valley of the two lakes).
Returning to **Laragh** and turning right we follow signposts for **Rathdrum**. Halfway along this road on our left, we see the smallest village in Ireland, **Clara,** with it's church, school and two houses. Continue through the attractive village of **Rathdrum** where Ireland's 19th century leader, *Charles Stuart Parnell,* lived on the nearby **Avondale** Estate. We continue through the delightful Wicklow countryside via **Aughrim, Tinahely** and **Shillelagh.**
Leaving Wicklow we enter Ireland's second smallest county, Carlow.We pass through the town of **Tullow** on the river Slaney and head for Carlow town. About 1 km berfore Carlow town we follow signposts for the **Browneshill Dolmen,** situated on a ridge overlooking the Barrow. This massive dolmen, erected over 4000 years ago, is the largest in Europe and is estimated to weigh over 100 tonnes.
Returning to the main road we continue on to **Carlow town,** a bright, modern town with a fine Catholic Cathedral completed in 1833. The town's courthouse is by the celebrated *Sir William Morrisson* and it has a Doric potico modelled after the Parthenon in Athens.
The main road takes us on our final 30 kms of this tour to one of the finest cities in Ireland, **Kilkenny**. The city, situated on the *River Nore* has many notable attractions. Following signposts for the city centre and heading up *John Street* we pass on our left Edward Langton's award-winning pub/restaurant. Continuing over the river we head for **Kilkenny Castle**. A guided tour of this exquisitely furnished 13th century castle, home to the *Dukes of Ormonde* for over 500 years, is available. Take a stroll in the 20 hectares of parkland adjoining the castle.
The tourist office in the restored 16th century **Shee Almshouse** in Kieran Street will supply a map of the city and also offers a view of mid 17th century Kilkenny in its *Cityscope model.*
We stroll down *High Street* and see some of the finest traditional shop fronts in Ireland.

Kilkenny is also a good centre for buying Irish crafts. Also in High Street are the 18th century **Tholsel** (city hall), the beautiful 16th century residence called Rothe House, now the museum of the dKilkenny Archaelogical Society and the 18th century courthouse. Further on is the second largest cathedral in Ireland, **Saint Canice's** (13th century) with the impressive tombs of *Piers and Margaret Butler* (Ormonde family) on the right hand side as we enter the cathedral.Climbing to the top of the round tower in the cathedral grounds we get a fine view of the surrounding area.

TOTAL DISTANCE: 195 KMS
PUBLIC TRANSPORT :
DUBLIN/KILKENNY : Regular bus services from Busarus and regular rail service from Heuston Station in Dublin.Tél. (01) 366111
DUBLIN/GLENDALOUGH :
St Kevin's Bus Service departing from St. Stephens Green , Dublin.
Derartures twice daily Tél. (01) 2818119

WEXFORD - WATERFORD

"Through a region rich in outstanding historical monuments, castles and abbeys, museums, nature reserves, forest parks and gardens".

Wexford town stretches along by its silted up harbour with the statue of *John Barry, "Father of the American Navy"*. Its charming Main Streets (north and south) preserve many traditional shop fronts. Beside **Wetgate Tower** is a stretch of the old city wall, the *"Tom Moore Tavern"*, one of the oldest pubs in Ireland, and the twelfth century ruins of **Selskar Abbey.** Leaving Wexford we take the **R733** to **Wellington Bridge**, turning off left after 6km for **Johnstown Castle**, built in 1840 and now headquarters of the agricultural institute. The castle itself cannot be visited but

the grounds, with fine views, statued walkways, exotic trees can be visited on weekdays.
7km from Wellington Bridge a left turning leads by a very narrow road to **Tintern Abbey**, a Cistercian monastery founded in 1200 by *William Marshall, Earl of Pembroke*, on the spot where he was washed up after a shipwreck. The monastery was later converted into a private house by the *Colclough* family, who continued to live in it until 1958. It is now in the care of the state. 8km further on, past **Arthurstown**, a turning left leads to **Ballyhack**, a charming ferry village with the remains of a 16th century tower house. This road is unsuitable for heavy loads due to very steep inclines. After a further 6km we see **Dunbrody Abbey**, one of the most imposing Cistercian monuments in Ireland. Founded in 1182 and dissolved in 1536 the ruin is worth visiting for its church with transept chapels, chapter house and refectory. Approx 7km further on is the **John F Kennedy Memorial Forest Park,** an aboretum covering 194 hectares with 3000 of trees and shrubs and a fine visitors' centre constructed of cedar and local stone. A deviation left leads one by pot-holed roads to **Dunganstown** and the humble ancestral home of the *Kennedy* family, now a farmer's shed.

Newross is a pleasant port on the *River Barrow.* The road to Waterford follows the river at first and then goes up onto wooded hill country offering fine views back over the river.

Waterford (40 000 population) is Ireland in miniature. It has an old town with narrow streets and a modern industrial quarter, home to *Waterford Glass* and *Ray-Ban* sunglasses. It has elegant shopping areas with splendid cathedrals as well as dilapidated and run-down sections. There are still some fine remnants of its city walls including the Viking **Reginald's Tower,** now the city museum.

Half day Tour: Leave **Wexford** northwards by the **N11**. After 6km we cross the river *Slaney* estuary and enter at **Ferrycarrig** the **Irish National Heritage Centre** which has reconstructions of a crannóg, burial sites, round towers, motte and bailey and many other typical buildings. Continuing north to **Enniscorthy** which has a 16th century castle, now the local museum, a dominating red-bricked psychiatric hospital *St Senan's*, and a fine cathedral by the noted architect, *A W Pugin*. Taking the **N79** and continuing with the *Blackstairs* mountains on our right to **New Ross**. At New Ross join the **N25** to **Waterford**.

Irish National Heritage Park,Ferrycarrig, Co. Wexford

TOTAL DISTANCE 67km
Wexford/Waterford - Buses 3 times daily.
Wexford/Enniscorthy - buses 3 times daily.Enquire; Bus Eireann, Redmond Square Wexford.

CORK - BLARNEY - KINSALE

"A day of castles, a magic stone, and a ghost"

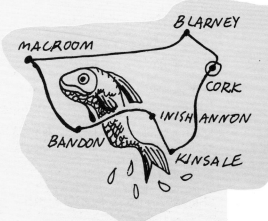

Leaving **Cork** from the *Lady"s Well Brewery*, we cross a hill and descend into *Blarney Valley*. Surrounded by groves of yew and holly (said to have been used by the druids for worship) the massive fifteenth century keep of **Blarney Castle** appears. Here *Cormac Laidir MacCarthy* rescued a drowning girl who told him then of a magic stone in his castle: he had only to kiss it and all powers of eloquence would be his. *Cormac MacCarthy* used it to great effect, for his evasive answers to *Queen Elizabeth's* demands for submission eventually provoked from her to burst out

"*This is all Blarney!*", thus adding a new word to the English language. Nowadays it is an essential duty for any active tourist to kiss the stone. The McCarthy's lost Blarney after the Reformation Wars, and the succeeding owners built the fine mansion open to the public close by. The village had a thriving woollen industry until the recession of the 1970's; it is now famed for its shopping facilities.

Proceed past the *Blarney Park Hotel* towards **Macroom**. After emerging onto the main road, we pass a dam and power station on the *River Lee*. The view is impressive, but much obscured by trees. Above the dam the river swells into a lake. Turn south at **Coachford** for **Bandon**, crossing a bride over the lake.

We enter **Bandon** passing by *Kilbrogan Church*. This was reputedly the first Protestant church built in Ireland, and the town stocks and whipping post are still on display here. Bandon was founded by the *Earl of Cork*, an adventurer in the days of *Queen Elizabeth the 1st* of England who took over enormous tracts of land from Cormac MacCarthy and others. Some fragments remain of the town walls.

We go down the *Bandon River* now, past the ruined **Dundaniel** and **Kilbeg castles** to **Inishannon**, and thence past the ruined castle of **Poulnalong** to Kinsale.

Kinsale was a Norman town and harbour. It had much trade with *Spain*, and many pilgrims making the great medieval pilgrimage to *Saint James of Compostella* in *Spain*. Kinsale first achieved prominence, however, in 1601, when *Spanish forces* landed here to aid the Irish in their last great struggle against *Queen Elizabeth of England*. The English forces managed to prevent the Spaniards from linking up with the Irish army, and eventually the Irish surrendered and the Spaniards sailed away. **Kinsale** today is a charming town, with a fine marina and lovely medieval lay-out. **St Melrose's** is a beautifully preserved parish church of the 13th century, with the town stocks in the porch and some fine Vicotorian stained glass. Kinsale is also Ireland's *"gourmet capital"*, noted particularly for seafood.

Outside of Kinsale is the well-preserved, star-shaped **St Charles' Fort**. It is haunted by a woman in white, the daughter of the fort's governor, who killed herself on her wedding night because her father had mistakenly shot her newly-wedded husband.

The return trip to Cork takes us past **Cork Airport,** recently much expanded in a programme to improve regional air transport facilities.

Kinsale

TRAVEL DISTANCE : 63 Km
PUBLIC TRANSPORT: Regular bus service from Cork to Blarney, and from Cork to Kinsale. Check at the bus station, Parnell Place, Cork.

CORK - KILLARNEY (VIA GLENGARIFF)

"Mountains, bays and gardens make an enchanting trip to Killarney".

Leaving **Cork** along the south bank of the *River Lee*, a massive Victorian psychiatric institute frowns down at us. We pass a few commuter villages and come to a large lake, created by the building of a hydro-electric dam on the River Lee.

Shortly before **Macroom** we turn off into rougher countryside. Left of us the Lee flows

through a myriad intertwining channels in a low swampy forest. This ecologically unique area of the **Geeragh** was once the home of the brigand, *"Sean Ruadh" ("John the Red")*, and his faithful dog.

Deep in the mountains lies **Gougane Barra** where *St Finbar,* patron saint of Cork, built a monastery after ridding the lake of a monster. In its flight to the sea the monster carved out the Lee Valley.

We continue through the narrow **Pass of Keimenagh,** once leaped over by a stag. Finally we descend to **Bantry Bay**. Here the patriot, *Wolfe Tone*, tried to land with a French fleet in 1796, but was driven off by bad weather. A large oil terminal was used in Bantry Bay by Gulf Oil, but was closed after 50 people were killed in an explosion in 1979.

From **Glengarrif** we can take a trip on a boat to the magical gardens on **Garnish Island,** then continue over the dramatic **Caha Pass** to **Kenmare.**

In order to pay his soldiers with land, the English dictator, *Cromwell*, commissioned *Sir William Petty* to carry out the first survey of Ireland. Recognizing iron ore in this area, Petty founded the town of **Kenmare** to work it. A stone circle here can easily be visited on foot.

We now cross **Moll's Gap** into the **Black Valley**. At **Ladies' View**, where *Queen Victoria* of England and her ladies climbed out of their carriages to admire the view, we see the long Upper Lake which runs out through the Long Range to the two other lakes, Muckross Lake and Loch Leine.

To the left looms **Carrauntouhil**, Ireland's highest mountain, (1,038metres); right of this the **Gap of Dunloe** gives access to the lowlands beyond.

The oakwoods in the valley are a remnant of the ancient forests of Ireland. Notice the moss and ferns growing on the trees. Holly abounds here, and strawberry trees (arbutus), native otherwise to the Mediterranean, grow by the lakeshore. Both are being crowded out by

Bantry Bay

rhododendrons and are now being burned away.

Muckross House, a large house on the shores of **Muckross Lake**, now belongs to the Irish government.The main rooms are in their original style, while items of Kerry folkcrafts are displayed in the basement. The gardens are superb.

Killarney is surrounded by mountans and lakes and has been the main tourist attraction of Ireland since early in the last century. It has not lost any of its Irish character on that account. The **Cathedral** is a fine work of *Pugin*, the main architect of the English and Irish neogothic.

DISTANCE : 98 km.
PUBLIC TRANSPORT : Daily bus service from Cork to Killarney via Glengarriff. Check at the Cork Bus Station, Parnell Place.

KILLARNEY - THE RING OF KERRY

"The Iveragh Penninsula, known as the Ring of Kerry, celebrated for its natural beauty, rich in history and literature, a marvel for the traveller to behold".

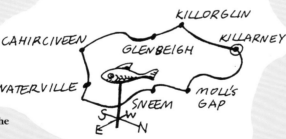

Our tour begins from **Killarney,** celebrated for its beauty and natural idyllic setting between lakes and mountains.

We leave Killarney via the *Killorglin road*. In the distance lying off to our left we can see the **McGillicuddy Reeks** with Ireland's highest mountain, **Carrantuohill** (1038metres) wreathed in mist.

Killorglin, our first town on the ring of Kerry is chiefly known for *Puck Fair*, the annual horse and cattle fair which has become a major tourist festival, attracting visitors in search of music and dance. The custom of crowning a goat (poc in Irish) of the fair is thought to go back to pagan times, the month of August or Lughnasa when the

fair is held having connections with the *Celtic God Lug*. Killorglin is also an excellent place to find smoked or fresh salmon. From here the road continues inland through pleasant countryside with a fine view at *Caragh Bridge*. Here we can spot an old railway bridge, the first of many reminders of the now defunct line between Farranfore and Valentia Island, closed since 1960. We continue towards **Glenbeigh**, the valley of the birch trees, considered by early travellers to be the last outpost of civilization. Near here is **Rossbeigh**, famed in legend as the beach from which *Oisin*, poet, musician and warrior rode off on a white horse with *Niamh* of the golden hair to the land of perpetual youth - Tir na nOg. We can now see **Dingle Bay** and the **Slieve Mish** mountains beyond to our right. From here we travel inland to Cahirciveen, passing a turf-burning power station on our right. Just before **Cahirciveen** still on the right are the barely recognisable ruins of the birthplace of **Daniel O'Connell, the Liberator** who gained the final civic liberty for Catholics when he was allowed to take his seat in parliament at *Westminister* in 1829. In **Cahirciveen** we see the church built to commemorate the centenary of his birth in 1875.

From Cahirciveen we turn southwards by passing **Valentia Island**, once famed for its smuggling activities, which lies out to our right in the ocean. We pass through open countryside and arrive at **Waterville** where the famous actor *Charlie Chaplin* spent holidays with his wife *Oona*. As the road rises out of Waterville we can take in the fantastic view out to sea and if visibility permits, see the striking **Skellig rocks** rising out of the ocean. The small Skellig is a nesting ground for gannets whilst the greater, **Scelilig Mhicil**, is one of the finest monastic sites in Ireland but almost inaccessible.

We climb further to a viewing point known as **Coomakista** from where we get a breathtaking view of the Atlantic, the *Kenmare* river and the *Beare Penninsula* to the south. Travelling eastwards we look to the right for the stone fort or 'cathair' which gives the next village **Caherdaniel** its name. We pass a signpost pointing to **Derrynane House**, former home of **Daniel O'Connell** which is now a museum and national monument.

We continue towards **Sneem**, stopping to view **Staigue Fort** - a magnificent example of a stone fort whose walls, in which there are rooms and staircases, are about 4 metres thick and 6 metres high. As it has not been excavated it is difficult to date, but it may have been built about 2000 years ago and was probably a royal residence.

Passing the white strand at **Castle Cove,** we go inland to **Sneem** which proudly announces to visitors that it was winner of the Tidy Towns competition in 1987. This most attractive and unusual village is divided into the curiously named north and south square (in reality triangles) by

Derrynane Harbour

Sneem River which flows at this point over fascinating rock formations. The *Anglican church* is probably best known for its weather-vane in the form of a salmon, recalling at once the profusion of fish nearby and the early Christian symbol.

Sneem has no less than three monuments to the late *President Cearbhaill O'Dailaigh* who returned to live here in 1976 after resigning from the presidency. He died here in 1978 and is buried in the local graveyard. The first monument known as the *'Steel Tree'* was presented by the president of *Israel Chaim Herzog* who is of Irish origin and this sculpture is in North Square. The second is in South Square and is an abstract work by Irish sculptor *Vivienne Roche*; the third at Quay Road is a white marble panda bear presented by the Chinese people.

Travelling from Sneem to meet the main Killarney/Kenmare road at **Moll's Gap,** we pass through wild and desolate countryside of extreme beauty. From **Moll's Gap** we descend a winding road overlooking panoramic vistas of the lakes blow and the mountains surrounding them to **Killarney.**

TOTAL DISTANCE: 165km
PUBLIC TRANSPORT : Daily bus services between Killarney and Cahirciveen. Tours of the ring available from local operators. Please check at Killarney railway station or local tourist office.

LIMERICK TO GALWAY VIA THE BURREN

A day of dramatic sea cliffs and "lunarlandscape".

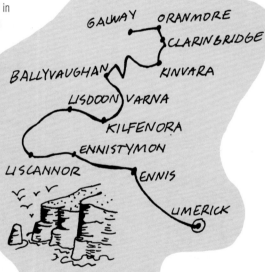

Not far outside of Limerick lies **Bunratty castle,** main seat of the *O'Brien* lords. This has been renovated in the style of its hey-day, the age of *Queen Elizabeth I* of England, and medieval banquets are held daily in it. The surrounding *folk park* is well worth visiting.

We go through **Ennis**, county town of County Clare, and on to colourful **Ennistymon.** Lovely paths have been built for strolling along the waterfalls here.

Soon we see three ringforts to the right, dwelling places of the affluent around the time of Christ's birth. Just before us is **Lahinch**, a seaside resort developed in the last century and was served by a now defunct narrow gauge railway. The

championship golfcourse here is extremely difficult. A sunken city lies out in the bay: *" he who sees it has but two weeks to live."*

On the left we see the modest ruins of the church of *St Macreehy*, an early Christian saint who saved his people from a giant, corpse-eating eel. Sand from his grave makes even the stormiest seas as smooth as glass.

Soon after **Liscannor**, the remains of *Cornelius O'Brien's Arabian palace* are visible. It is now inhabited by a farmer and his cows. The pillar on the slope behind is a monument to Cornelius, erected at his command and paid for by his impoverished peasantry. Next to it is the holy well of *St Bridget*.

The spectacular **Cliffs of Moher** host many bird colonies. *Kittiwakes* and *fulmar petrals* nest on the cliffs, below are *puffins*. The people here used to descend on ropes to collect eggs and fledglings. **Warning! The cliff edges are very dangerous!**

Our journey now brings us past **Lisdoonvarna** with its mineral springs and spa to **Kilfenora.** Beside the late *Romanesque cathedral* here are two well-preserved *High Crosses*. **Kilfenora's Burren Centre** offers a good introduction to the **Burren.** We continue to *Leamaneh*, an O'Brien castle and home of strong-willed *Maire Ruadh*, and on into the **Burren.**

The **Burren** is in many ways a paradise. Warm-loving plants from before the Ice Age (eg maidenhair fern) mix here with alpine plants from the Ice Age (gentians and mountain avens). Round about stretches the naked bedrock. Here sits **Poulnabrone**, a dolmen from the Neolithic. Another somewhat later *megalithic grave* lies about one kilometre further on. We can visit one of the many caves riddling the Burren at **Ailwee,** just before Ballyvaughan. **Ballyvaughan** is the Burren's harbour, and the *Martello Tower* in the bay was built to fend off *Napoleonic invasion*.

We now drive along the edge of the bay, past **Kinvara** and the **Castle of Dun Guaire** (so frequent and lavish were the gifts *King Guaire* gave, that his right hand grew longer than his left). *Medieval banquets* are celebrated here as in Bunratty.

The famous beds of *native oysters*, consumed enthusiastically by gourmets from around the world at the *oyster festival* every September, lie near **Clarinbridge.**

After the *Norman castle* at **Oranmore** we reach the edge of **Galway city**.

TOTAL DISTANCE: 103km
Travel TImes: Limerick to the Cliffs of Moher 1 1/2 hours.
Cliffs of Moher to Kilfenora: 20 minutes

Cliffs of Moher

**Kilfenora to Ballyvaughan 1 hour
Ballyvaughan to Galway 1 hour**

**PUBLIC TRANSPORT: Buses twice
weekly via Lisdoonvarna and
Ballyvaughan to Galway. Check at
Colbert Station, Parnell Street, Limerick.**

GALWAY - CLIFDEN

*"A full day trip through South Connemara,
an ever-changing landscape of lakes and
streams, thatched cottages snuggling under
hills. The blue of the sea and (occasionally)
of the sky mingles with the brown of bogs,
the mottled green or marble, the red of
fuschia, purple of rhododendron and the
grey mottled coat of the Connemara pony. A
place to be photographed, understood and
enjoyed for its legends and stories".*

Leaving **Galway**, the **N59** follows the
River Corrib leading to *Lough Corrib,*
the largest free fishing waters in Europe.
Crossing the river we see on our right
the ruins of **Menlo Castle**, home of

John Blake, a nineteenth century high liver.
He applied for election to Parliament in
order to gain immunity from his creditors
and received the news of his election on a
boat on the river where he was sojourning
to avoid the process servers. Half-way to
Moycullen on your right is **Drimcong
House**, which has an *Egon Ronay* star and
won, in 1990, the supreme award as the
best restaurant in Ireland. In **Moycullen**
itself on your left is the *Connemara Marble*
factory where you can tour and see the
working of different types of marble, one of
Ireland's most popular gifts.

14km further on a signposted turning to the
right leads to **Aughnanure Castle**
(unfurnished) a typical 16th century tower
house, now a National Monument. From its
roof a view can be had of the battle between
the fishermen and their prey on **Lough
Corrib**. Further on (3km) is the village of
Oughterard, the major fishing centre for
the lake. In a thatched bar on its main street
many tall tails are told about fish, life and
even about the lake itself. It is said, for
example, to have an island for every day of
the year - 365 (and 366 in a leap year).

Leaving Oughterard, lakes appear left and
right of the road, low hills, cottages and
everywhere the bog, that wet brown mass of
compacted vegetation. Turf workings appear
with the dug sods drying in large and small
stacks under sun and wind. From time to
time along the road are signs of the old
Galway-Clifden railway line and sometimes
an even older transport - horse and cart,
just like the one *John Wayne* used in the
film *"The Quiet Man"*, which in 1952
popularised the region. At **Maam Cross** is
a replica of the cottage used in the film,
which you can visit free.

Clifden

Twenty kilometers further on is the
signposted turning onto the **R341**. This
wooded road leads down to **Ballynahinch
Castle**, formerly centre of the largest
private estate in Britain and Ireland - over
250,000 acres - now a luxury hotel. It's said
about the original owner, *Richard Martin,*
that when his friend, the *Prince Regent,*
boasted about the length of the avenue at
Windsor, Martin replied that his avenue was
fifty miles long - the road from Galway.
Martin was known as **"Humanity Dick"**
for his founding of the *Royal Society for the
Prevention of Cruelty to Animals*. Tenants
who mistreated their donkeys ended up in
the prison on a little island which can still
be seen on Ballynahinch lake. For three
miles the road runs along the *Abhainn Mor,*
a river famous for its salmon. At the
Angler's Return pub, a road left leads to
Cashel where *General de Gaulle* holidayed
in 1969. Five miles further one comes to
Roundstone, a village with one or two
good seafood restaurants.

This beautiful stretch of road follows the
peninsula coastline and there are many fine
sandy beaches stretching out westward to
Slyne Head. Further west lies America and
there are two links with the New World here.
Just past **Ballyconneely** are the remains
of the wireless station established by
Marconi; further on, like a shark's fin on a
hill to the left, is the memorial to **John
Alcock and Arthur Brown**, two British
pilots who landed there on 15 June, 1919,
the first men to fly the Atlantic. The road
follows the coast from there on to **Clifden**,
the "capital" of Connemara, which has good
seafood restaurants and a good number of
hotels, hostels and guesthouses.

**TOTAL DISTANCE:110km
Route: Leave Galway north-westward
on the N59 and travel directly for 40
miles. Turn left onto the R341
(signposted Roundstone &
Ballynahinch Castle) and continue on
this coastal route 25 miles to Clifden.**

**PUBLIC TRANSPORT : Bus Eireann's
regular service leaves Galway for
Clifden every day at 18.00 (Thurs &
Sat 11.15) and travels on the N59
directly to Clifden. On Wednesday
and Fridays it follows the route
outlined here.**

89

CLIFDEN GALWAY VIA LEENAUN

"Through the heart of North Connemara by mountain and sea, a trip though untouched regions. Beautiful panoramas of hill, field and lake where the eye stretches for miles without a sign of other people".

We leave **Clifden** by the chapel and head directly north along the **N59,** or alternatively by the Alcock and Brown hotel and out for a beautiful drive along the **Sky Road** (signposted). **Clifden** is a centre for the breeding of the *Connemara pony,* a small sure-footed cross-breed, excellent for jumping and with children. It brings good luck to see a Connemara pony on your way; see seven and you can have a wish come true. A viewpoint 6km from Clifden gives a panorama of north Connemara. A further 8km from here is the entry to **Connemara National Park** where *Irish red deer* are being reintroduced. Just before this entry is one of the best craft shops in Connemara selling tweeds, woollens and other craft produce. Pass through the village of **Letterfrack,** a former *Quaker* settlement, and after 3km turn left at the post office and in to **Kylemore Abbey,** a beautiful house built in the 1870s by a Manchester magnate, now a girls' college run by the Benedictine order. Observe high on the hillside the white statue commemorating Holy Year. A lakeside walk leads to the chapel where the original owner and his wife are buried. (The Abbey makes its own pottery which can be bought in the excellent craft shop).

Leaving Kylemore, a profusion of *rhododendrons* accompany the visitor along the road to Leenaun. At 8km a turn left leads to **Rosroe** and the *youth hostel,* formerly the residence of *Ludwig Wittgenstein,* known locally as *"The Professor".* Straight on leads along Ireland's only fjord, **Killary Harbour**

with its mussel beds, to **Leenaun,** in whose only hotel *King Edward VII* of England holidayed in 1903. The village has recently found stardom again as the setting for the film **"The Field",** a story of land hunger and murder. Here we turn right to approach **Maam Valley (R336)**.

This valley between the **Twelve Bens** (right) and the **Maumturk Mountains** (left) is the kingdom of the sheep, who wander freely over it. Each sheep bears a mark indicating the proprietor. Further south the road begins to rise; extensive views are available over **Lough Corrib** and its many islands. Note on one of those islands **Castle Kirk,** a stronghold of *Grace O'Malley,* the pirate queen. Legend tells of a tunnel under the lake leading away from the castle, but no such tunnel was found by the antiquarian *Sir William Wills Wilde,* whose house, *Moytura,* was a favourite with his son *Oscar.* **Moytura House** now belongs to *Bono,* the lead singer with the group U2. Just outside **Cong** village are the imposing walls of **Ashford Castle,** once a home of the *Guinness* family, now a luxury hotel. Beside the castle are the charming ruins of 12th century **Cong Abbey.** Further on is the village of **Cong,** where *"The Quiet Man"* was shot. The village is situated between Loughs Corrib and Mask. During the 1840s a canal was dug to join the two lakes. Unfortunately, as limestone is porous, it simply drained away. The "Dry Canal" is just north of Cong.

2km from **Cong** turning right onto the **R334,** we continue to **Headford,** passing the well-preserved ruins of the **Franciscan Ross Abbey.** At Headford join the **N84** and head directly southwards along a perfectly straight nineteenth century toll road known as the *"New Line".* Note the lack of habitation along it. Before coming into Galway notice on your left **Ballindooly Castle,** recently restored by its American owner. Our journey ends at **Galway.**

TOTAL DISTANCE: 117KM

ROUTE: North from Clifden on the N59 to Leenaun (34km). Right at Leenaun and thence down the Maam Valley to COng (R336 branching into R345). From there joining the N84 to Galway.

PUBLIC TRANSPORT: The CLifden-Galway service leaves every day at 08.00 and usually goes directly eastward on the N59. On Tuesdays and Thursdays however it follows the route suggested above. Journey time 2 1/2 hours.

Kilemore Abbey

GALWAY - ACHILL ISLAND

"Through scenic countryside to religious sites and magnificent seascapes".

We leave **Galway** on the *Tuam Road.* At **Claregalway** we pass the ruins on the left of a *de Burgh castle,* on the right a thirteenth century *Franciscan Friary.*

Tuam is the ecclesiastical capital of Connaught. Its **Church of Ireland Cathedral** was probably founded in 1130 by *Turlough O'Connor,* but only the chancel with its triplet window and chancel arch survive from this period. The shaft of the High Cross in the nave perhaps belonged originally to the Market Cross in the square. Both bear an inscription to Turlough O'Connor and a contemporary abbot. The **Market Cross,** signed by a Leinster artist, resembles the

High Cross at Glendalough.

When *Pope John Paul II* visited Ireland in 1979, it was primarily to come to **Knock** for its centenary celebrations. In the depressed years at the end of the last century, in a countryside which, of all Ireland, had been worst ravaged by the *Great Famine* thirty years before, a vision of the Virgin, St Joseph, St John the Evangelist, and an altar with a lamb and cross appeared against the church wall. Today the Basilica (affiliated with San Maria Maggiore in Rome) open air facilities, and road systems demonstrate Knock's importance. Incoming pilgrims are further facilitated by the airport north of town.

The county town of Mayo is **Castlebar,** a well-built town with a large square and tree-lined mall. Its greatest day was the day of the *"Castlebar Races"* in 1798, when *General Humbert* and his mixed French and Irish forces routed the British army. *John Moore* was thereupon proclaimed President of the Provisional Republic of Connaught, a presidency which ended one week later when Humbert was forced to surrender at Longford.

Next on our route is **Westport** town, an eighteenth century gem, with a gracious tree-lined mall and formal octagon. *Westport House* has magnificent collections, including the long-missing pillars from the tomb of *Atreus in Mycenae* (originals now in the British Museum). Beyond the town rises the mass of **Croagh Patrick**, where *St Patrick* banished the snakes forever from Ireland. Extra trains are laid on to Westport for the pilgrimage up this mountain at the end of July.

In **Newport** we visit the *neo-Romanesque Catholic* church to see its magnificent stained glass window by *Harry Clarke*. Glaciers once surged over this land, and their last spasms left

swarms of little gravel hills everywhere. They are all around us, and march out into **Clew Bay** as innumerable islands. In these intricate waters *Graineuaile (Grace O'Malley),* a notable female pirate, learned seamanship. We pass **Carrigahooley Castle**, where she divorced her husband by shouting "I dismiss you" as he tried to enter. Nearby are the ruins of the **Dominican Burrishoole Abbey**.

We cross the bridge at **Achill Sound** onto **Achill Island**. During the oil shortages of World War II a thriving shark fishing industry existed here, exploiting the huge but harmless (plankton-eating) basking sharks that surface here in June after winter hibernation in the muds offshore. Much experimentation proved that the oldest means the most effective : netting the sharks and then harpooning them from curraghs! *Keel Strand* is the longest of Achill's idyllic beaches. Further west, amethysts are found on the southern slope of *Croaghaun*. To the north is another superb beach at **Dugort.**

TOTAL DISTANCE:118km
PUBLIC TRANSPORT: Daily service Galway via Castlebar to Westport, and Westport to Achill Island.

SLIGO - A TOUR OF YEATS' COUNTRY

" Through a countryside immortalised in the writing of W B Yeats, Nobel Prize winner in 1923, and captured on canvas by his brother Jack B Yeats, a countryside which they thought of as the 'Land of Heart's Desire".

Sligo is a county of extraordinary beauty and vivid contrast in its lakes and forests, mountains and rivers. It is a county that has so much more to offer than could ever be captured by pen or canvas. We begin our tour from **Sligo** town, situated at the mouth of the *Garavogue* river and surrounded by mountains - **Benbulben**

(526m) and **Truskmore** (645m) to the north; the **Ox Mountains** to the east and **Knocknarea** (329m) to the south.

Leave Sligo on the *Dublin road* forking to the left approx 1km past the *courthouse and garda barracks* (signposted *Tobernalt*). Shortly we catch our first glimpse of beautiful **Lough Gill** and the **Garavogue River**. We also see part of **Hazelwood** estate. **Hazelwood House** is one of the largest Georgian houses in the county and the estate can be entered from the northern shore of Lough Gill. Approx 200m further on we find the entrance to the car park of **Cairns Hill Forest Walk.** Two hills here, **Belvoir** and **Cairns** are crowned by two stone cairns of the passage tomb types.

Continuing on our route we take a short detour at the next right hand turn to the **'Holy Well'**, signposted **"Tobernalt"** This was an important ancient Celtic assembly site of *Lughnasa* festivities in honour of the Celtic

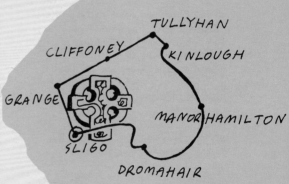

god Lug who gave his name to the Irish form of the month August. The well water is attributed with many cures.

Returning to the lake road and turning right we soon note **Dooney Forest Walk** and nature trail. Walking along the lake shore and up a steep climb we get some magnificent views of Lough Gill and the mountains surrounding it. Short detours can be made off the main *Dromahair road* to **Cashelore** stone fort and to the lake shore to get a close view of the lake isle of *'Innisfree'*, immortalised in the poem by W B Yeats.

On arrival at **Dromahair** we note that we are now in **Co Leitrim**. Dromahair is a pretty village resting in wooded surroundings on the banks of the *Bonet*

Achill Island

River. Not far from the village we find a prominent rock plateau from whose lofty heights Lough Gill and its islands provide a breathtaking view. Also to visit at Dromahair is **Creevelea Abbey** founded in 1508 and situated on the left bank of the Bonet River. We continue along the eastern shore of the lake and head through the picturesque and wild countryside of north Leitrim to **Manorhamilton,** a modest rural town. From Manorhamilton, we make our way towards **Kinlough** through the **Valley of Glenade**, famous for its rare scenic beauty, this wild and rugged district has captivated many a traveller. Here we are in 'sheep country'.

Shortly after Kinlough, which is a major angling centre, we reach **Tullyhan,** Leitrim's only seaside resort lying on the coast overlooking the broad Atlantic where the three counties of Donegal, Leitrim and Sligo meet.

92

We turn towards Sligo and approx 50m before **Creevykeel** crossroads, we note the signpost and entrance to **Creevykeel court tomb.** This is the finest example of a classic court tomb, with full court, in Ireland. The tomb was built between 3,000 and 3,500 BC.

From Creevykeel crossroads we take a detour to **Mullaghmore** where we find a fabulous sandy beach running for 3km. In the background towering above the beach and village is majestic **"Classiebawn" Castle,** former home of the last *Viceroy of India*, the *Earl of Mountbatten.*

Lying off Mullaghmore is the island of **Inishmurray,** uninhabited since 1947.It is the most southern breeding ground of the *Eider* duck.

Returning to the **N15** we travel to **Cliffoney** and then to **Grange.** Shortly after which we leave the main road yet again to visit **Lissadell.**

Lissadell House was once the home of the *Gore-Booth's.* Ancestors include *Sir Henry Gore-Booth* (1843-1900), the arctic explorer, and *Constance Gore-Booth* (1884-1927), a leader in the 1916 uprising and sentenced to death by the British. W B Yeats stayed here and referred to Lissadell many times in his writings. Lissadell is open to the public in summer and its estate is now a forestry and wildlife bird reserve.

Rejoining the main **N15** at **Drumcliffe,** we pause at this picturesque village nestling beneath Benbulben and it is here in a lonely churchyard we find the tomb of the great **W B Yeats** (1865-1939). Poet, patriot and Nobel Prize winner, we recognise his tomb by the now famous epitaph of his own composition -

Glencar Lake

"Cast a cold eye on life, on death, horseman pass by".

Whilst in Drumcliffe, (which was an important Christian monastic site founded by St Colmcille in AD 575), we visit the round tower and see the 10th century high cross, the only one known to occur in Co Sligo.

We return to **Sligo** via **Rosses Point**, a favourite seaside resort with two magnificent sandy beaches, situated 8km from Sligo.

**TOTAL DISTANCE: 76 miles.
PUBLIC TRANSPORT : Daily services between Sligo/Manorhamilton. Tullaglan/Sligo. Bus Eireann organised tours of Lough Gill and Yeats country available. Contact Sligo Tourist Office.**

DONEGAL - WEST AND NORTH WEST COASTLINE

"An everchanging spectacle of stunning landscapes and seascapes set against a backdrop of mystical mountains and moors".

Our tour beings from **Donegal Town** which is situated at the estuary of the *River Eske* as it flows into **Donegal Bay**. Donegal gets its name from the fact that the Vikings established a fort here (Dun na nGall - Fort of the Foreigners) and it later came into

prominence as the chief seat of the great warrior clan, the *O'Donnell's,* who were forced into exile by the English around 1607. Today Donegal town is famous for its idyllic setting and its tweeds.

Our journey first takes us out along the northern shore of Donegal bay to the village of **Mountcharles** situated on a hillside overlooking the bay. We drive through fertile land to **Dunkineeley** and onto **Killybegs,** a major centre for the Irish fishing industry. Although it was granted borough status in 1616 by *King James of England*, today it looks very much like a late Victorian village built around a good harbour. The arrival of the fishing fleet and the unloading of the catches

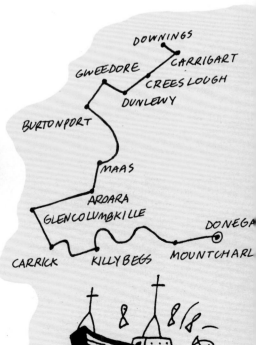

Errigal Mountain

for the gourmet restaurants of Ireland and Europe is a sight worth seeing and an experience to remember.

From Killybegs, we make our way further along the bay to **Kilcar,** a centre for the handwoven tweed industry and then onto **Carrick** set on good land above **Teelin Bay.** Carrick is an excellent base for climbing the spectacular **Slieve League** which rises some 600m from the sea forming the highest marine cliff in Europe.

We travel onto **Glencolumbkille** where the soil becomes poorer but the scenery nevertheless remains breathtakingly beautiful with its typical Donegal blend of hills and sea. Glencolumbkille is named after *St Colmcille* (Columba of Iona) and there seems little doubt that the man himself spent time here and set up a monastery. Many legends associated with the saint are retold by the locals. Worth visiting nearby is a *Beefan* (1km away), an early ecclesiastical site. There is a small chapel inside a stone-walled area which has a number of cairns and cross-slabs with some evidence of geometric designs. Nearby we find **Colmcille's Well.**

From Glencolmbkille, we make our way through wild and desolate countryside of immense beauty. This area makes up one

of the largest Gaelic speaking communities (Gaeltacht) in Ireland. We stop in **Ardara,** an important centre of Donegal handwoven tweed and handknits produced from a thriving cottage industry. Here we have the opportunity of seeing hand looms in operation.

Continuing on the **N56** we travel to **Maas** on *Gweebara Bay*. This area is dotted with magnificent sandy beaches. We make our way northwards to **Dungloe,** known as the capital of **The Rosses**. This is a lake and rock strewn district with houses dotting the poor soil and the people Gaelic speaking. This area is geologically interesting and west of Dungloe there is a megalithic portal tomb at **Roshin South.**

Lying out in the majestic Atlantic is the island of **Aranmore** that has been inhabited for many thousands of years. The island is readily accessible from **Burtonport** and has good cliff scenery in the north-west.

After Dungloe we drive through The Rosses to **Gweedore.** Situated in spectacularly wild countryside, it is a major holiday centre and the area is renowned for game fishing due to the *Gweedore* and *Clady rivers*.

Veering east at Gweedore we travel towards **Dunlewy** lying under the

shadow of **Mount Errigal**. This road offers remarkable scenic beauty by Lough's *Nacung* and *Dunlewy* into the *Derryveagh* mountains with Errigal's (750m) white quartzite cone rising like a miniature *Fujiyama*.

From Dunlewy we take the national park road and visit **Glenveagh National Park** lying deep in a gorge formed at the base of high surrounding ridges by geological action.

Lough Veagh is a beautiful long, narrow lake running along the bottom of the gorge for some 8km. Surrounded by mountains and woodland, a castle has been strategically placed to offset the natural beauty. Built in 1870, the castle with its surrounding 10,000 hectares changed hands many times until it was presented to the nation during the 1980's by the last owner, Henry P McIlhenny. Today it is a must on the traveller's trail through Donegal.

Leaving the National Park we travel to **Creeslough** situated at the head of **Sheephaven Bay** and continue on towards **Carrigart.** At *Doe Castle*, we pause and admire this 15th century keep of the O'Donnell clan which is sea protected on three sides and by a deep fosse on the fourth. Nearby, we see **Muckish** (610m), Donegal's third highest peak and not an easy one to climb.

Travelling on to **Carrigart,** we leave Gaeltacht country behind us. Carrigart is situated on an inlet of **Mulroy Bay** and in the sandhills between it and **Downings** there are many prehistoric habitation sites where numerous objects of the Bronze Age have been found.

Downings (famous for its tweeds) is a fine village in a most idyllic setting looking out onto the waters of Sheephaven Bay with imposing but impressive Muckish in the background. It boasts some of the finest beaches and it would be impossible to exaggerate the beauty of it and nearby *Rosguill Peninsula* with its breathtaking Atlantic drive.

TOTAL DISTANCE: 200km
PUBLIC TRANSPORT: Buses run between Donegal town and Glencolmbkille, Donegal Town and Killybegs, and Donegal town and Dungloe. This trip is not easily done by public transport.

FACTS AND FIGURES
A TRAVELLERS GUIDE

GETTING ACQUAINTED

CLIMATE

Lying roughly at the same northerly latitude as Newfoundland, it has a mild moist climate due to the prevailing south-westerly winds and the influence of the warm gulf stream along its western and southern coasts. With no part of the island more than 70 miles from the sea, temperatures are fairly uniform over the whole country.

Average air temperatures in the coldest months January and February are mainly between 4 and 7 degrees Centigrade. The warmest months, July and August, have average temperatures between 16 and 18 degrees Centigrade but occasionally reaching as high as 26 degrees Centigrade.
The sunniest months are May and June with an average of 5 5 to 6 5 hours a day over most of the country.

LANGUAGE

The Republic of Ireland has two official languages, English and Irish (Gaelic). English is spoken everywhere and although most people know Irish it is only the 83,000 or so inhabitants of the western Gaeltacht areas that use Irish as an everyday language. All official documents are in both languages. Likewise so are all road and town signs.

TELEPHONES

In the Republic, telephone services are operated by the state owned company, Telecom Eireann. You will see the Irish word "Telefon" over all street cabins (of which there are many). Public telephones are also located in hotels, public houses (pubs) and some shops. Instructions are written in French, German and English.
A local call from a public telephone cabin costs 20p. Longer-distance calls can be dialled direct as can international calls. Area codes are listed in the front of telephone directories. Dial 10 for operator assistance. Telephone services in Northern Ireland are operated by British Telecom. Dial 100 for the operator.

POPULATION: 3.6 MILLION
RELIGION: ROMAN CATHOLIC
SIZE: 70,882 sq km

AGE STRUCTURE
0-13 years	38%
14-28 years	15%
29-45 years	24%
46-75 years	23%

LABOUR FORCE: (000's) 1,350

THE IRISH ECONOMY
GNP (£M)	1991	24,250
EXPORT OF GOODS AND SERVICES (£M)		16,657e
IMPORTS OF GOODS AND SERVICES (£M)		14,285
GNP GROWTH (in real terms)		3.6% (1991)
INFLATION		3.75%(proj)
WAGE INFLATION		3.75%(proj)
INTEREST RATE		14.25%

BANKS

Opening hours: Monday - Friday 10am - 12.30 / 13.30 - 15.00. On Thursdays the banks stay open until 17.00.

POSTAL SERVICES

At the time of writing, letters weighing less than 20 grammes cost 32p within Ireland and to all EEC countries. Postcards cost 28p. All post offices are open Monday - Saturday from 9am until 5.30pm with the exception of the General Post Office on O'Connell Street in Dublin which is open till 11pm.
You will notice that the best way of recognising post offices is by the Irish words "Oifig an Phoist".
Stamps can also be bought from hotel reception desks.
In Northern Ireland, British postal rates apply.
Remember that you cannot use stamps from the Republic in Northern Ireland and vice versa.

NEWS MEDIA

The Irish devour newspapers as they are great political animals. There are no fewer than six daily newspapers serving the island's population of five million.
The Irish Times, the Irish Independent and the Irish Press are published in Dublin. The Times is the most serious and comprehensive and is best for foreign news, arts and business. The Independent has a hard-hitting style and is a very popular paper while the Press is newsy but less brash.
The Cork Examiner is the staple diet of business and farming people in the south-west whilst in Belfast one finds the Unionist/Protestant News Letter and the Nationalist/Catholic Irish News.
There are four evening papers and five Sunday papers. Local papers (there are 100) can provide you with useful information on regional news and goings-on.

RADIO AND TELEVISION

The national broadcasting service, Radio Telefis Eireann (RTE), has two TV channels and two radio stations. In addition there are numerous independent radio stations and all British TV channels can be received throughout most of the country. The Irish speaking areas of the western seaboard have their own radio station - Radio na Gaeltacht.

HEALTH AND EMERGENCIES

Visitors from EEC countries are entitled to medical treatment in Ireland and should obtain Form EIII from their National Social Security office. These forms entitle the owner to free treatment by a doctor and free medicines on prescription. If hospital treatment is necessary, this will be given free in a public ward.

For emergency services such as Garda Siochana (police), ambulance, fire service, lifeboat and coastal rescue, telephone 999 (in either part of Ireland) and ask for the service you need. Other useful numbers are: Poisons Information Service, Dublin - 379966; Lost Property - (Trains only) Dublin - 363333; Dublin Dental Hospital: 01.6794311.

Pharmacies (chemists) are open from 9am till 5.30pm, Monday to Saturday, with some open from 11am to 1pm on Sundays. French Embassy, 36 Ailesbury Road, Dublin 4. Tel: 2694777; German Embassy, 31 Trimleston Avenue, Booterstown, Dublin. Tel: 2693011; Italian Embassy, 63 Northumberland Road, Dublin 4. Tel: 601744; British Embassy, 31 Merrion Road, Dublin 4. Tel: 2695211 American Embassy, 42 Elgin Road, Dublin 4. Tel: 688777 Australian Embassy; Wilton Terrace, Dublin 2. Tel: 761517 Canadian Embassy, 65 St. Stephens Green, Dublin 2. Tel: 781988

TOURIST OFFICES

There are some 70 tourist offices located throughout the country which are generally open from 10am until 6pm. For further information contact the Irish Tourist Board - Bord Failte, in Upper O'Connell Street, Dublin. Tel: 747733.

TIPPING

In hotels and restaurants, a 15% services charge is normally added to the bill as a tip. No added tip is required except in the case of exceptional service. Tipping is not normal in bars unless there is table service. 10% is the usual tip for a taxi and 50p per bag for a porter.

TRAVELLING TO IRELAND (GETTING THERE)

BY AIR

Ireland has three international airports: Dublin, Cork and Shannon, and five national airports: Waterford, Farranfore, Galway, Sligo and Knock. Regular flights are available from most major European and UK cities and from New York, Boston and Atlanta in the US. Some direct flights from UK cities to the national airports are available. However internal connecting flights from Dublin are readily available.

BY SEA

Many ferries connect Ireland to Britain and France. These include: Rosslare (Co Wexford) to Fishguard and Pembroke (Wales), Cherbourg and Le Havre (France), Cork to Le Havre and Roscoff (France), Dun Laoghaire (Dublin) to Holyhead (Wales), Dublin to Holyhead (Wales), Larne (Co. Antrim) to Stranraer (Scotland). Details of services and operators are liable to change. For full details contact a travel agent.

TRAVELLING IN IRELAND (GETTING AROUND)

TRAINS

Irish Rail - Iarnrod Eireann operates trains to cities and towns throughout the country. Trains are clean, modern and efficient. There are two classes - standard class (2nd class) and Super Standard Class (1st class). Standard class one way fare - Dublin - Cork £31.50 Dublin - Galway £24.00 Dart (Dublin Area Rapid Transit), the electric suburban railway serves 25 stations along the coast from Howth in North Co Dublin to Bray in Co Wicklow. Further information on 01.366222.

BUSES

Irish Bus - Bus Eireann has a nationwide network of buses serving all the major cities and most towns and villages outside the Dublin area. It also provides services in Cork, Galway, Limerick and Waterford. The minimum adult fare is £2.00; Child's fare (under 16) is £1.00, half the adult rate.

Dublin Bus - Bus Ath Cliath controls all public bus services in the greater Dublin area (which includes parts of Wicklow, Meath and Kildare) as well as the Dart feeder and commuter services. Minimum city bus fare is 55p. Note: Most city bus services are one-man operated with no conductor so have correct fare ready if possible.

AIRPORT BUS SERVICE

Dublin Bus operates bus services between Dublin Airport and the central Bus station (Busarus). Buses depart every twenty minutes from early morning to midnight. The adult fare is £2.50, children £1.25.

Irish Bus operates a bus service from Cork Airport to the city and also from Shannon Airport to Limerick. The service operates every thirty minutes during peak periods and every hour off peak. Adult fares: Shannon - Limerick £4.50 return, £3.40 single. Cork Airport - City centre £2.50 return, £1.70 single. Children half price.

Special Rail and Bus Passes
Rambler Pass
CIE, The national transport company, offers 8 and 15 day passes for unlimited travel on bus and train. Tickets can be bought at any bus or train station in Ireland,

or prior to departure through a travel agent or CIE International Tours in your city.
Rail and Bus, 8 days - £78
15 days - £115
Rail or Bus, 8 days - £60
15 days - 90
Children under 16 years - half the adult fare.

Emerald Card
This pass provides unlimited bus and train travel in the Republic of Ireland and Northern Ireland.
15 days - £180   8 days - £105.
For further details, contact Dublin (01) 366222.

EURAILPASS

Ireland is a member of the Eurail network and EurailPasses are valid for all provincial bus and train travel in the Republic of Ireland. A free ferry link is provided by Irish Ferries from Le Havre and Cherbourg in France to Rosslare or Cork. These tickets must be bought in advance from offices of the participating railways.

NORTHERN IRELAND

For rail information contact Belfast Central Station (Tel: 230310). Bus information may be got through Ulsterbus, Belfast (Tel: 220011).

TAXIS

There are metered taxis at railway stations, ports and airports in Dublin, Belfast, Cork, Limerick and Galway. Elsewhere, fares are by arrangement with the driver in advance. In cities and towns you can book a taxi by telephone. If a taxi is ordered there may be a pick up charge.

DRIVING / CAR HIRE

Touring by car is the most popular way to get around and can be a real pleasure as the roads here are the least congested in Europe.
Driving on the left is the rule both in the Republic and in Northern Ireland. Drivers and front seat passengers must wear seat belts.
In the Republic, the speed limit is

48km in urban areas, and on country roads 88km.
In Northern Ireland the limit for country roads is 96km and 112 km is allowed on motorways and dual carriage ways. A valid international driving license is required. Most major car rental companies have Irish operations. By prior arrangement most car hire companies allow cars to be taken into Northern Ireland from the Republic. Manual cars are the norm but automatic transmission is available at a higher cost.
For environmental reasons, Ireland, like many other countries, is encouraging its motorists to use unleaded petrol. There is now a network of filling stations throughout the country where unleaded petrol is available. A list of these stations is available from the Irish Tourist Board.
Car rental companies will only rent to drivers between the ages of 23 and 70 years. Company policy varies so it is best to check before making reservations.
Motorcycles and mopeds are not available for rental.

NB In the larger cities it is advisable to ensure that no items of value are left on view in the car when parking.

COACH TOURS

Many companies offer completely escorted coach tours, varying in length and itinerary.
Full day and half-day guided tours are also organised from the larger towns and cities to the most

interesting and scenic spots. These normally run between May and October.

CRUISING ON INLAND WATERWAYS

The river Shannon is navigable for approx 150 miles downstream from Lough Key in Co Roscommon. The other two main waterways for cruising are the Grand Canal which runs westward from Dublin across the central plain to the Shannon, and the River Erne, navigable for 50 miles from Belturbet, Co Cavan, all through upper and Lower Lough Erne to Belleek, Co Fermanagh. All three waterways are marvellous for photography, fishing, bird watching, rowing or just getting away from it all. There are eleven approved companies which offer cabin cruisers in the Republic, nine on the Shannon, one on the Grand Canal and one on the Erne.
In Northern Ireland, seven companies operate for the Erne. Cruisers range in size from two berths to eight. All have refrigerators, gas cookers, hot water, showers and dinghies, charts and safety equipment are all included. Experience in handling a boat is an advantage, but instruction is provided for novices.
Details from respective tourist boards.

ISLAND BOAT SERVICES

Off the west coast, one finds a series of small and unusual islands, each with its own

particular charm. Boat services operate to most of these islands from the local mainland. A regular boat service, taking three hours, operates from Galway to the more famous Aran Islands. Aer Arann, operating from the outskirts of Galway, has several flights daily to Aran and takes just 30 minutes.

IRISH COASTAL FERRIES

There is a 30 minute car ferry across the River Shannon from Tarbert in Co Kerry to Killimer in Co Clare. The ferry leaves Killimer every hour on the hour and Tarbert every hour on the half hour.
There is a 10 minute car ferry across the Suir river, operating continuously and taking one hour off the driving time between Ballyhack, Co Wexford and Passage East in Co Waterford.

COUNTY CLARE

This mid western county contains a rich textured variety of landscapes, from the jagged coastline and lunar like appearance of the Burren in the northwest to the soft rolling pastures of the Shannon estuary area.

Clare is rich in historic relics and is marked with the signs of a tempestuous past. Dotted throughout the county are some 2,300 stone forts dating back to pre-Celtic times. Hundreds of castles, such as Bunratty are also a reminder that this was the land of the great Gaelic chieftains, the O'Briens of Thomond.

Clare is often the first county visited by Americans as they touch down at Shannon airport. Opened in 1945 as the first duty-free airport in the world, it has attracted many foreign based companies to its surrounding industrial estates. This in turn has provided the region with jobs, greater prosperity and confidence. Clare people have traditionally made their living from farming and fishing but the county is probably best renowned for being a celebrated centre of authentic traditional music. Throughout the county one can find pubs with live music and dance and in particular such towns as Doolin, Miltown Malbay, Ennistymon and Liscannor are hives of activity with music lovers coming from all over the globe in the summer months.

Tourism plays an important part in the economy of the county but as yet Clare remains relatively wild and unspoilt. In the northwest of the county is the dramatic Atlantic coastline around the Cliffs of Moher. The Burren which overlooks the Aran Islands and Galway Bay is a strange and beautiful karst landscape where hundreds of rare species of flora and fauna survive in the fertile limestone soil. The Burren area extends for some 40km from east to west and 24km from north to south. Throughout the area there are many cavern and cave systems which have been formed by underground rivers. Probably the most well known of these is the Ailwee Cave near Ballyvaughan which dates back to 2 million BC. At the edge of the Burren is the spa town of Lisdoonvarna which is a popular resort especially in September when a matchmaking festival is held. Spinsters come from as far away as the USA to participate in the fun! Other important festivals and events are held throughout the county. In late May, Ennis, the county town, hosts the Fleadh Nua, a festival of traditional music, dance and song. One of the most celebrated music summer schools is the Willie Clancy Summer School which is held in Miltown Malbay in early July. Clancy (1921-73) was a musician, folklorist and master carpenter. He was noted for his beautiful renditions of traditional Irish slow airs on the uilleann pipes, an instrument that he was considered to be a great master of. The summer school, which lasts for ten days, consists of lectures, recitals, concerts and music sessions and attracts musicians from all corners of the globe.

NOTE: For quick and direct access to County Kerry, take the Killimer/Tarbert car ferry accross the Shannon Estuary.

CLARE:
Population: 90,826
Land Area: 1251 sq. miles/
3,238 sq. km
ENNIS:
Population: 5,917
Distance from:
Dublin - 142 miles/228km
Cork - 87 miles/140km
Shannon - 14 miles/22km
Rosslare - 150miles/241 km
Rail Service: No Service.
Airport: Shannon International
Airport (061) 61444
TOURIST OFFICE:
Shannon Airport:
(061)61664 All Year
Ennis:
(061)28366 All Year

VISITS & ACTIVITIES

AILLWEE CAVE,
BALLYVAUGHAN, CO. CLARE
Tel: (065) 77036
Fax: (065) 77107
The ideal start to your holiday in the Burren is a leisurely tour underground in Ireland's premier showcave. Tours every ten minutes from 10am to 6pm. Appetizing food prepared in their own kitchen is served in the Cave's award winning building which also houses a distinctively different craftshop. Afterwards watch the cheesemaker at work producing Burren Gold cheese in the farmhouse produce shop. An experience not to be missed!

RESTAURANTS & PUBS

O'CONNOR'S PUB
DOOLIN, CO CLARE
Tel: (065) 74168

Established 1832. This delightful family run pub is internationally known for its friendliness and hospitality. Famous for traditional music and song!

Scrumptious bar food served daily from 12 midday to 8.45pm. Specialising in mussels and mouthwatering beef and guinness stew. Last stop before you visit the Aran Islands.

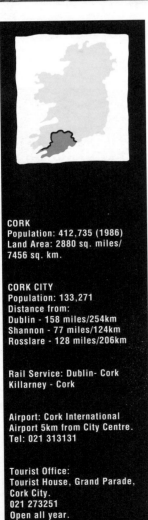

CORK
Population: 412,735 (1986)
Land Area: 2880 sq. miles/
7456 sq. km.

CORK CITY
Population: 133,271
Distance from:
Dublin - 158 miles/254km
Shannon - 77 miles/124km
Rosslare - 128 miles/206km

Rail Service: Dublin- Cork
Killarney - Cork

Airport: Cork International
Airport 5km from City Centre.
Tel: 021 313131

Tourist Office:
Tourist House, Grand Parade,
Cork City.
021 273251
Open all year.

Cork is the country's largest county and it is also the Republic's second largest city. In the north of the county is some of the richest agricultural land in the whole of Europe - the fertile Golden Vale. In the south-west are the rough beautiful peninsulas of Mizen, Sheep's Head and Beare, offering superb coastal and mountain scenery with semi-tropical vegetation due to the influences of the Gulf Stream.

Just south of Cork city is the important port of Cobh from where many Irish emigrants departed to seek their fortunes in the New World. Further to the west is Ireland's gourmet capital, Kinsale.

County Cork is an ideal place to indulge in relaxing pastimes, as it boasts some of the finest hotels and restaurants in the country as well as numerous pubs with colourful clientele. For the keen sportsman the county offers a wide choice of activities such as sailing, deep-sea angling, salmon and trout fishing, horse-riding and golf. For those in search of culture, Cork has numerous stately homes and gardens and ancient castles, the most famous of which is unquestionably Blarney, just five miles to the north-west of the city. In the days of Queen Elizabeth I, the castle was held by Dermot McCarthy, who had the gift of plamas, the Irish word for soft, flattering or insincere speech. The Queen had asked him to surrender his castle, but he continued to play her along with fair words and no action. The frustrated Queen is supposed to have said "It's all Blarney - he says he will do it but never means it at all". Today, "Blarney" is synonymous with colourful, persuasive language and has found a place in the Concise Oxford English Dictionary.

Cork City lying on the banks of the River Lee is a popular tourist destination. Its name comes from 'Corcaigh', the Irish word which means the marshy place. The city stands on marshes originally created by the river. These marshes were drained and the river diverted into two smaller streams which run around the city centre, which is an island.

Cork with its 19thC skyline and fine opera house is generally regarded as the cultural capital of Ireland. As the second largest city, with a 150 year old Victorian University, it has engaged in an age-old rivalry with Dublin. Both cities can trace their roots to antiquity but Cork's founder is generally considered to be St Finbar. During the 6thC, Finbar established a monastery where the Gothic spires of the cathedral bearing his name now stands. With the arrival of the Vikings in the 9th century, everything was virtually destroyed. The Danes returned however to establish their own settlement which expanded once the agricultural potential of the surrounding fertile land was known. The modern city of Cork was officially founded by a charter from Prince John in 1185, three years before Dublin. This was the source of considerable civic pride when it celebrated its 800th birthday in 1985.

Cork people are famed in song and story, and no little feared, for their shrewdness. Dubliners, envious of Corkonians natural business skills, describe Cork as being 'God's own place with the devil's people'.

Cork people can be proud of having produced a cosmopolitan centre humming with energy and confidence.

Cork plays host to some of the country's best festivals. In May there is the Cork choral festival. In June the Film International Festival, in September the Mobil Irish Rally is held and later in October the city is crowded again for the Guinness Jazz Festival.

Life in the country moves at a more leisurely pace. Those living in the Golden Vale are primarily involved in dairy farming and stud farms. In the south, quite a number of people commute to Cork, to work in the various large industries established such as brewing and computers. Tourism is vitally important both in the city and in the west Cork areas where the land is rugged and holdings are small.

Crosshaven on the Cork harbour estuary is the playground of Cork businessmen and their families and is one of the country's leading centres for yacht enthusiasts. The Royal Cork Yacht Club has its base here; the Royal Cork is the oldest club of its kind in the world having been founded at Cobh in 1720.

Skibbereen is the gateway to the most southerly of the Cork and Kerry peninsulas, places of astounding beauty for the visitor but where life is hard for the small farmers who toil the barren land. In stark contrast to the rugged and barren mountainous scenery are such balmy resorts as Bantry and Glengarriff, to name but two of the coastal towns. Lying just off Glengarriff is Garnish Island, whose large collection of subtropical plants is unrivalled anywhere else in Ireland. George Bernard Shaw spent time here.

For Irishmen and tourist alike, Cork is an exceptional county of contrasting scenery and lifestyles. It is a true microcosm of all Ireland!

ACCOMMODATION

**INNISHANNON
HOUSE HOTEL**
INNISHANNON, CO CORK
Tel: (021) 775121
Fax: (021) 775609

"The most romantic hotel in
Ireland". Built in 1720 as the home
of a prosperous farmer,
Innishannon House retains its old
world charm of that era.
Completely refurbished in Irish
country house style and run with
flair by your hosts, the O'Sullivan
family. Its ambience is
reminiscent of a petite chateau in
rural France. Set in 4 hectares of
parkland and riverside gardens,
on the banks of the Bandon River
(renowned for its salmon fishing).
Daily fresh fish arrivals are
prepared with flair by our brigade
of Irish and continental chefs.
Superb cellar. All rooms en suite
with TV, direct dial phones, radio
and central heating. Fishing, golf,
squash, tennis and woodland
walks all nearby.

**THE MILLS INN
BALLYVOURNEY (N22)
MACROOM, CO. CORK**
Tel: 026-45237
Fax: 026-45454

"Real Ireland for Less"

This is one of Ireland's oldest
award-winning country inns
offering first class food and
accomodation (all rooms en-suite
with full facilities £16pps).
Situated half-way between Cork
City and Killarney on N22 it is an
ideal location for fishing, golfing,
forest walks or touring Cork/Kerry
region.

Open all year around. Museum,
Art Gallery, landscaped gardens
featuring castle ruins.

VISITS & ACTIVITIES

**FOTA WILDLIFE PARK
CARRIGTWOHILL
CO CORK**
Tel: (021) 812678 / 812736

Walk through grassland where
giraffes and antelope roam,
through woods where wallabies
rest, past bird-filled lakes and
monkey islands. 70 species from
5 continents. Tour Train, Coffee
Shop. Ten miles from Cork city
(turn for Cobh from RT N25).

STAY ON AN IRISH FARM

A farmhouse holiday is more than
just another holiday – it is an
experience, full of warmth,
kindness and caring.
It is a feeling of belonging and
sharing the traditions of Irish
home life with the families who
have, for generations, farmed the
land of Ireland.

Informality is the keynote, and the
sense of quiet brings relaxation
which is so much needed by so
many people today.
Spend one night, one week.
Have bed and delicious Irish
breakfast and if you wish, you
may order a home cooked evening
meal before 12 noon any day.
Further information and illustrated
guide* available from:
Mrs. Martha O'Grady
Glynch House
Newbliss, Co. Monaghan
Tel: (047) 54302

* Illustrated Guide incl. postage
STG£3.50, cheque must
accompany request for guide.

99

COUNTY DONEGAL

DONEGAL
Population: 129,664 (1986)
Land Area: 1869 sq. miles/
4839 sq.km

LETTERKENNY:
Population: 6691
Distance from:
Dublin - 146 miles/235km
Cork - 280 miles/450km
Shannon - 207 miles/333km
Rosslare - 248 miles/400km

Rail Service: No service

Airport: Carrickfin Airport
Tel 075 48284
8km from Dungloe.

Tourist Office:
Derry Road,
Letterkenny,
Tel 074 21160
Open all year.

Some regard Donegal (Dun na nGall - Fort of the Foreigner) as the 26th county in a 25 county state, meaning that there is an individuality and independence up here that Dublin prefers to ignore.

This Ulster county has the largest number of native Irish speakers in Ireland. The dialect spoken here has more in common however with highland Gaelic than with the southern strain. Indeed there are great links with Scotland and many districts of Glasgow are reputed to be like parishes of west Donegal. This was the county most affected by the partition of the country. The eastern part of Donegal, where the land is good and the landscape dull, has a high proportion of Protestant farmers and shopkeepers who look towards Northern Ireland - its natural hinterland. For many living in this area, Derry was their regional capital. These people regarded Derry and Glasgow as places rooted in their oral tradition, for many of them were descendants of planter families that came over from Scotland in the 16th and 17th centuries. The people in the south Donegal did not feel so isolated by the border. They turned naturally to Sligo - their hinterland.

In the far west of the county is the officially recognised Irish speaking area - the Gaeltacht - where government grants encourage people to stay put. The locals speak English with a soft and poetic lilt as though through translation they have made a second language of it. The people who lived in the cottages of the lonely sheep glens of the Gaeltacht area once used to pass the evenings weaving Donegal tweed and pass the time singing and composing poetry. Donegal is still the county of tweed and a large cottage industry has been created around it especially in the area west of Donegal town around Ardagh and, in the far north, around Downings.

Like in most western seaboard areas, Donegal has a tradition of emigration, especially to Scotland. Nowadays the government grants available encourage people to remain. The current baby boom is being experienced in this county more than anywhere else. This makes up for rural depopulation which has scourged the countryside since the famine of 1845-58. The new generation are not being brought up on the old homesteads but in new cottages along the roads near the factories that the government has enticed here with substantial assistance.

Donegal is a county of endless beauty, rugged and wild, melancholic and dramatic. Its mountain ranges are older than any other in Ireland. In the south one can savour the wide expanse of Donegal Bay. Donegal Town is an excellent centre for touring this area and just west of it is Killybegs, the major fishing port on the west coast.

Lying just north-west of here is the Gaeltacht and the area of the Rosses. Dramatic Atlantic coastline interspersed with heathery glens, russet boglands, endless lakes and majestic mountains create one of the most beautiful areas of Ireland.

As one travel further north the area of mountain and sea is interlinked with breathtaking views around Mount Errigal, Mount Muckish, the towns of Falcarragh, Creeslough, Carrigart and Downings. Hidden behind Errigal is the Poisoned Glen. There are many tales surrounding the origin of its name, some saying that the water in the lough is unfit to drink because of poisonous plants at the water's edge.

The Fanad Penninsula Scenic Drive is a "must". The views of Lough Swilly are breathtaking and the 3 mile long sandy beach at Ballynastocker Bay (voted one of the "top 10 Beaches in the World" by Observer magazine) is as spectacular as it is free from people.

Donegal is a county steeped in history and legend. Passing through Letterkenny, administrative centre and famous for its folk festival, held every August, one reaches the countryside where St Columba spent his first years. (St Columba or Colmcille was the great Irish missionary who founded a church at Iona, Scotland). Nearby is the National Park at Glenveagh, where Irish red deer and peregrin falcons nest.

The county's most important archeological site is on the Inishowen Peninsula and is called the Grianan of Aileach. Grianan means a sun-palace. It is a unique stone fort built about 1,700 BC and was at one time the residence of the kings of Ulster. From the top of Grianan one can see Lough Swilly from where the Gaelic Aristocracy fled to France in 1607. This event is known as the 'Flight of the Earls'. Further to the south of the county is the important Lough Derg, visited by thousands of pilgrims each year.

ACCOMMODATION

**SHANDON HOTEL
MARBLE HILL STRAND
PORT-NA-BLAGH
VIA LETTERKENNY
DONEGAL**
Tel: (074) 36137
Fax: (074) 36430

A most beautifully situated hotel set in own grounds with grass tennis court, 9 hole pitch & putt and children's play area.
The comfortable lounge introduces a friendly and homely atmosphere.
50 of the 55 bedrooms (incl. 8 family units) overlook Marble Hill blue flag beach, with wind surfing school and canoes for hire.
A family owned hotel, we pride ourselves on our excellent cuisine and the personal attention which we give to all our guests. Children are welcome with excellent reductions, over 60's discount on weekly and 5 day holidays (May, June, Sept., Oct.).
Indoor swimming pool for 1993 season. Dublin 264 km, Galway 272 km, Belfast 194 km
Grade A Hotel.

**RATHMULLAN HOUSE
RATHMULLAN, LOUGH SWILLY
LETTERKENNY, CO DONEGAL**
Tel: (074) 58188 / 58117
Fax: (074) 58200

A gracious country house set in award-winning gardens stretching down to a sandy beach. Downstairs, the rooms are period style. An elegant pavillion-like dining room is renowned for good food. Bedrooms vary in size and cost. Indoor swimming pool, sauna, steamroom and outdoor tennis. 4 golf courses nearby. Ideally situated to visit Glenveagh National park or for a day's outing to the Giants Causeway. Grade A.

101

102

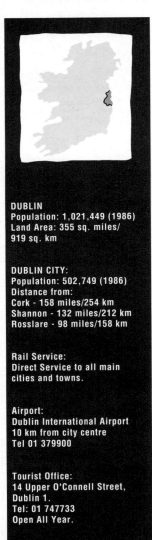

DUBLIN
Population: 1,021,449 (1986)
Land Area: 355 sq. miles/
919 sq. km

DUBLIN CITY:
Population: 502,749 (1986)
Distance from:
Cork - 158 miles/254 km
Shannon - 132 miles/212 km
Rosslare - 98 miles/158 km

Rail Service:
Direct Service to all main
cities and towns.

Airport:
Dublin International Airport
10 km from city centre
Tel 01 379900

Tourist Office:
14 Upper O'Connell Street,
Dublin 1.
Tel: 01 747733
Open All Year.

Dublin has a world-wide reputation for culture, wit, friendliness and beauty. Irish people call it affectionately 'Dear dirty Dublin', but this is a city that means many things to many people. For some it is a city of writers, for others it is a city of talkers, its pubs overflowing with Guinness and conversation. It is a city of many contrasts in a superb natural setting. Its streets can be full of bustle and yet places where people linger to watch the world go by. It is a city of elegant Georgian houses, run-down tenement flats and modern development centres all with their own attractive character.

Dubliners are a rare breed. They love to talk and tell stories like most Irishmen, but it is their sense of humour that is unique. The native Dubliner is jovial, quick-witted and can talk for hours about nothing in particular. One of the best places to meet a typical Dublin character is in one of the many pubs which are dotted all around the city.

One doesn't have to enter pubs however to catch a glimpse of the numerous 'characters' around Dublin. Moore Street, the open market just a short step from O'Connell Street, is full of them! Here the fruit and vegetable stalls are staffed by colourful and vociferous women who come mainly from the inner city areas. People often go just to hear the banter and badinage of the traders. A much loved character from Moore Street was Rosie - a plump, jolly woman who had a very quick tongue. One story recalls how Rosie replied to a woman who complained about the price of fresh mackerel: "What do you want for sixpence - Moby Dick?"!

Most Dubliners nowadays live in the suburbs that spread out into a large part of the county and commute to work in the city. The centre of the city is more commercial than residential. A great meeting place for young trendies is the stylish and elegant nerve centre of the south side - Grafton Street. This street is full of elegant upmarket shops, numerous eating establishments as well as traditional coffee houses such as Bewleys - from where the aroma of coffee wafts its way down half of Grafton Street.

It was just along the south side of the River Liffey that the Danes founded their first settlement in the 9th C. They built a garrison at the point where the River Poddle joined the Liffey to form a black pool or Dubh Linn, that gave the city its name.

North County Dublin boasts such scenic spots as Howth Head whose rugged brow overlooks the entrance to Dublin Bay. From the village one can walk to the summit around the nose of the promontory by a scenic cliff path. It is a fashionable place to live and nearby one can visit Howth Castle, the gardens of which are open to the public. There is a lovely story attached to the castle which concerns Grace O'Malley, the famous 16thC pirate queen from Co Mayo. She stopped in Howth to replenish her supplies of food and water and decided to visit the St Lawrence family, owners of the castle even to this day. The family were eating however and she was refused entry. Enraged by this rudeness, she snatched Lord Howth's infant son and heir and sailed away with him to Mayo. She returned the child only on condition that the gates of the castle were always left open at mealtimes, and a place set at the table for the head of the O'Malley clan. This custom is still kept!

Further along the coast is Malahide which is a seaside resort with a wonderful old castle. Just north from Malahide are the flat tidy fields of Skerries and Rush - two important centres for market gardening. Other places of interest in North County Dublin include Donabate, Balbriggan, Swords and Portmarnock, which boasts the country's most exclusive championship golf course, of international renown.

Travelling to the south of the county is Blackrock, a pleasant middle-class suburb overlooking the sea.

Dun Laoghaire is a Victorian-styled town from where the car ferry services leave for Britain. The town is called after the high king of Ireland who was converted to christianity by St Patrick! Not far from here is James Joyce's Tower at Sandycove. Now a museum, this tower was where Gertie McDowell showed Mr Bloom her garters in 'Ulysses'.

Further to the south is the lovely village of Dalkey where Bernard Shaw used to stay, and beyond that sweeps the beautiful bay of Killiney. In the background are the Dublin and Wicklow mountains where Dubliners go when they want to escape from it all.

County Dublin is quite small but can boast the country's capital at its centre, with some of the most splendid and diverse scenery on the east coast.

ACCOMMODATION

STEPHEN'S HALL HOTEL
14-17 LOWER LEESON STREET
DUBLIN 2
Tel: (01) 610585
Fax: (01) 610606
Sister hotels: Morrisons Island Hotel, Cork; Brennans Yard Hotel, Galway.

When you have tried conventional hotel accommodation, you'll find our suites more to your taste. Stephen's Hall Hotel is Dublin's only all-suite hotel. We offer exclusive accommodation, right beside St Stephen's Green, in the heart of Georgian Dublin. Our tastefully furnished suites have separate living rooms and fully equipped kitchens. All our suites are available for nightly or long-term stays and we provide free underground car parking.
The Terrace Restaurant in Stephen's Hall is open from 7.30am to 10.00pm and is popular locally for its intimate atmosphere and the quality of its food.
Reservations or information direct by phone, fax or post to the hotel. USA bookings or enquiries: 800-223-6510; Canada: 800-424-5500.

GEORGIAN HOUSE HOTEL
20/21 LOWER BAGGOT STREET
DUBLIN 2
Tel: (01)618832
Fax: (01)618834

This very comfortable 200 year old house in the heart of Georgian Dublin, only 150 yards from St. Stephen's Green and a 5-minute walk to all the major sites including Trinity College, galleries, museums, cathedrals, theatres

WHERE TO SHOP

MCCONNELL & NELSON
38 GRAFTON STREET
DUBLIN 2
Tel: (01) 774344
Fax: (01) 774284

McConnell & Nelson - your favourite smoked salmon and fresh fish supplier. Wholesale to hotels and restaurants. Worldwide delivery service.
Opening hours: Monday and Saturday - 9.00am - 13.00pm. Tuesday and Wednesday - 9.00am - 17.00pm. Thursday and Friday - 9.00am - 18.00pm.

and the fashionable shopping streets and pubs. All rooms have a bathroom en suite, direct dial telephone, TV. It is the perfect location for business or holiday travellers and offers all the amenities of an exclusive small hotel at guesthouse prices. Private car park, family rooms and seafood restaurant with Irish music at night.

PORT VIEW HOTEL
MARINE ROAD
DUN LAOGHAIRE, CO DUBLIN
Tel: (01) 2801663
Fax: (01) 2800447

Warmly welcoming! Relax, wine and dine by open turf fire with traditonal Irish music. Restaurant and bar. Situated two minutes walk from trains to Dublin, and ferry.

MOUNT HERBERT HOTEL
BALLSBRIDGE, DUBLIN 4
Tel: (01) 6684321
Fax: (01) 6607077

Mount Herbert Hotel is situated in private gardens in the heart of Ballsbridge, a quiet Dublin suburb with tree-lined avenues and elegant houses. This family run hotel is just a few minutes from the RDS, Lansdowne Road and many well-known Dublin pubs and restaurants. There are more than 100 well-appointed bedrooms and spacious parking facilities. For reservations, telephone (01) 6684321, fax: (01) 6607077 or write to Mount Herbert Hotel, Ballsbridge, Dublin 4, Ireland.

CLEO IRELAND LTD
18 KILDARE STREET
DUBLIN 2
Open all year round.
Tel: (01) 761421
Also: 2 Shelbourne Street
Kenmare, Co Kerry
Open April-November
Tel: (064) 41410

Retail and wholesale. Cleo's is a family business, established 1936. We design our own clothing using themes from Ireland's past, in natural fabrics specially chosen and woven for us from pure wool and linen, in colours of the Irish countryside.

RESTAURANTS & PUBS

LES FRERES JACQUES
74 DAME STREET
DUBLIN 2
(BESIDE OLYMPIA THEATRE)
Tel: (01) 6794555
Fax: (01) 6794725

One of Dublin's foremost and well-loved French restaurants, which combines a great bustling atmosphere with wonderfully creative French food. Fresh seafood and fish every day, game and seasonal specialities plus a varied a la carte and table d'hote menu have earned many accolades for this fashionable restaurant.
4-course Dinner £20.00; set lunches £13.00 + £9.50.
Live piano music. Private dancing facilities.
Lunch Monday-Friday 12.30 to 2.30pm. Dinner Monday-Saturday 7.30 to 10.30pm.

THE OLD DUBLIN RESTAURANT
90-91 FRANCIS STREET
DUBLIN 8
Tel: (01) 542028 / 542346
Fax: (01) 541406

Situated in the heart of medieval Dublin, the Old Dublin Restaurant has a name which fits perfectly. The city developed from a Viking settlement and this tradition is upheld in the Scandinavian and Russian recipes, specialities of this restaurant and for which it is rightly famous.
Eamon Walsh, the chef, uses only top quality Irish meat, fish, vegetables and dairy products creating tasty meals for all pockets. The restaurant has two private dining rooms.
Lunch is served fom 12.30 to 14.15, Monday-Friday. Dinner from 19.00 to 22.00, Monday-Saturday. Closed Sundays and on public holidays.
To book, telephone the following numbers: (01) 542028 / (01) 542346 from 9.30.

THE OLD SCHOOLHOUSE
SWORDS, CO DUBLIN
Tel: (01) 8402846/ 8404160
Fax: (01) 8405060

Lunch: Monday - Friday. Dinner: Monday - Saturday.
Charming XVIIIth century country school restored by the Sinclair family, preserving the traditional style. It's famous for its wonderful food and relaxed atmosphere. Only 10 minutes from Dublin Airport. Average cost for one evening: IR£20 including wine. In the last two years it has been awarded the Irish Tourist Board Prize for excellence. All credit cards accepted.
Early bird menu - 6:30 - 7.30pm: £10.50; Mon-Fri. Lunch Mon.-Fri. and Sun.

THE TOWER RESTAURANT
(1ST FLOOR),
IDA TOWER
CRAFT & DESIGN CENTRE,
PEARSE STREET
(OFF GRAND CANAL QUAY)
DUBLIN 2.
Tel: 01/775655

Situated in the Grand Canal Harbour area of Dublin, this beautifully appointed self-service restaurant offers you traditional Irish home cooking in a cosy, friendly old world atmosphere. Extensive menu - 3 course lunch £4.95. Hot and cold food served all day - 8.00am to 6.00pm. This historic 17th century tower has 7 floors of Irish craft shops and studios. Supervised carparking.

KING SITRIC
THE FISH RESTAURANT
EAST PIER, HOWTH
CO DUBLIN
Tel: (01) 325235
Fax: (01) 326729

Located in the picturesque old fishing village of Howth; Dublin Airport, Dublin City 20 mins. Lovely sea-view. Specialising in fresh fish landed daily. Sole, Lobster, Turbot, Crab, Squid ... Dinner Mon-Sat: 6.30-11.00pm Seafood & Oyster Bar (May-Sept only) Mon-Sat: 12.00-3.00 Closed Sundays & Public Holidays.

103

VISITS & ACTIVITIES

**THE IRISH WHISKEY CORNER
BOW STREET,
DUBLIN 7**

A visit to Dublin would not be complete without a visit to the Irish Whiskey Corner. Enjoy our film (in French, Italian, German), visit our museum and unique shopping area. Enjoy a glass of Irish whiskey in our 1920's Irish bar and perhaps become a certified Irish whiskey taster, complete with certificate. Pub lunches also available, but like visits, must be booked in advance.

Public opening 11.00 am as well as 3.30 pm.
For reservations, telephone John Callely (01) 725566.
Admission IR£3.00 from Jan 1, 1993.

**NEWBRIDGE HOUSE &
TRADITIONAL FARM
DONABATE
CO DUBLIN**
Tel: (01) 8436534
Fax : (01) 8452528

Newbridge House was designed by George Semple and built in 1737 for Charles Cobbe, Archbishop of Dublin (1746-1765).
It is most famous for its Red Drawing Room, with its elaborate rococo plasterwork and its Museum of Curiosities – items collected by members of the Cobbe Family on their world-wide travels.

Newbridge Farm consists of pigs, cows, lambs, geese, turkeys and many more furry friends.

**MALAHIDE CASTLE &
MODEL RAILWAY
MALAHIDE
CO. DUBLIN**
Tel: 8452655

The Lords Talbot de Malahide lived in Malahide Castle from 1175 to 1975. The Castle contains a very fine collection of Irish Period Furniture and part of the Portrait collection from the National Gallery of Ireland and with its 16th century panelled Oak Room and Medieval Great Hall, it certainly brings you back in time! The Cyril Fry Model Railway is a rare collection of model trains and trams in motion dating back to 1832.

**ST. MARGARETS
GOLF & COUNTRY CLUB
CONFERENCE CENTRE
BUSINESS & GOLF COMBINED
THE PERFECT ENDING TO YOUR
CONFERENCE**

The First Tee of Dublin's best voted Parkland Course is only yards away.

LOCATION WITHIN MINUTES FROM DUBLIN'S INTERNATIONAL AIRPORT AND 20 MINUTES FROM CITY CENTRE

We are fully equipped to handle all your conference needs.

* Corporate Events
* Seminars
* Meetings
* Product Launch
* Exhibitions
* Training Courses

For further details:
Tel: 01/8640 400
Fax: 01/8640 289

104

Dublin City Car Parking

Dublin City offers a number of secure car parks situated throughout the city. They vary from custom built multi-storey and underground lots to off street surface parks. Custom built car parks offer 24 hour secure parking.

Rates vary from 75p to £1.25 per hour during daytime. All day rates are available from from £6.00 to £12.00 depending on location.

Visitors are advised to use secure car parking facilities provided in the city as on street parking can lead to theft of vehicles and belongings.

Luggage, valuables, cameras etc should, if left in your vehicle, be concealed in the boot or elsewhere. It is advised not to leave any item visible in your vehicle.

PARK RITE   **Dublin City Car Parking**   **I C P**

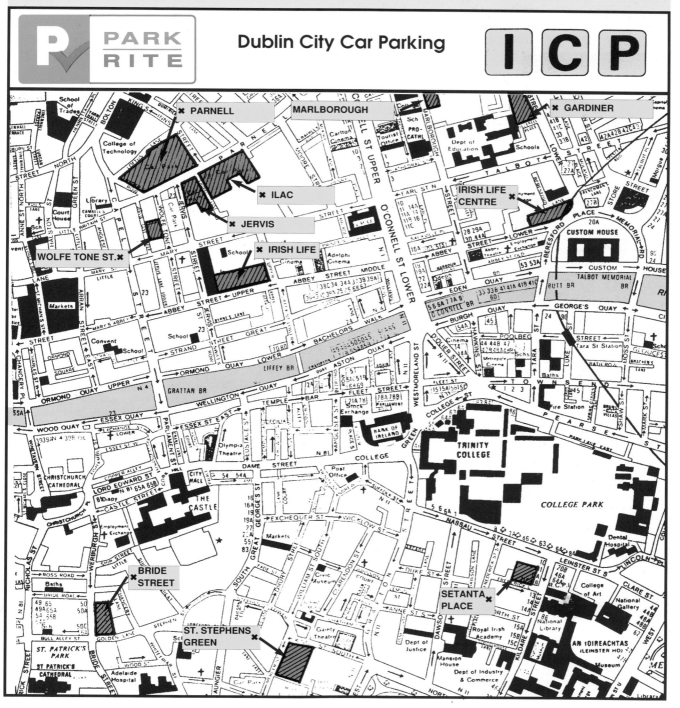

COUNTY GALWAY

GALWAY
Population: 178,552 (1986)
Land Area: 2374 sq. miles/
6146 sq. km.

GALWAY CITY:
Population: 47,104
Distance from:
Dublin - 135 miles/217 km
Cork - 128 miles/206 km
Shannon - 55miles/88km
Rosslare - 167 miles/269km

Rail Service:
Dublin - Galway City

Airport:
Galway Airport
8km from city centre
Tel: 091 55569

Tourist Office:
Eyre Square,
Galway City.
Tel: 091 63081
Open All Year.

Co Galway is the second largest county in Ireland and 50% of its population still speak Gaelic as their first language. It stretches from the wild and beautiful region of Connemara in the west to the banks of the River Shannon in the east. This a county of contrasts.

Bog and rich farming land extend east and north-east of Galway city. Towards the west along the windswept Atlantic coast and amongst the mountains of Connemara white-washed cottages tell of a different way of life. This is an area of stony barren ground which has seen many of its sons forced to emigrate to seek opportunities in far off lands. Most people nowadays survive by fishing, sheep farming and tourism.

Co Galway offers miles of lonely valleys, long beaches, excellent restaurants with delicious fresh seafood, colourful pubs with lively traditional music and friendly people. It is also an angler's paradise, boasting the largest inland lake in the Republic, Lough Corrib, as well as countless other lakes and the salmon filled rivers of Dawros and Owenglin.

Galway city is an attractive and prosperous administrative centre with a growing university, and with a particularly Irish atmosphere, which has attracted multi-national investment and has developed a vibrant industrial centre on its outskirts. It began as a small fishing village, but by the 13thC had become a walled and fortified town in the most sheltered corner of Galway Bay.

During the Middle Ages, the city of Galway enjoyed a prosperous business relationship with Spain and France. At this time it was ruled by the representatives of the 14 most prosperous families or tribes. It is still known today as the CIty of the Tribes.

County Galway is where myth is often as potent as history and the city itself is much given to creative folklore. One of the most famous tales is in relation to Lynch's Window. Here in 1493 Walter Lynch, Mayor of the city, hanged his own son for the murder of a Spanish guest. It was a crime of passion and such was the son's popularity with the people that no-one could be found to hand him. The Mayor was left to perform the hangman's task himself! The window is worth seeing and is only around the corner from the church of St Nicholas where Christopher Columbus alleged to have heard mass before leaving for America. The "evidence" for this is that one of his crew was known as William of Galway.

The city today is a thriving tourist centre and gateway to Connemara and the Aran Islands. During the summer months the streets teem with people from all corners of Ireland and all corners of the globe. Musicians play along the streets and farmers and their wives sell their produce in the marketplace.

Venturing west from the city one enters the Gaeltacht (Gaelic speaking) area of Connemara. This is an area renowned for its wild and rugged beauty. Inland lies some of the most beautiful and unspoilt landscape in western Europe which is very sparsely inhabited. Along the coast one can discover beaches of coral with a blue-green sea that resembles something from the Mediterranean. This is regarded by many as the 'Real Ireland' an area where natives cling to tradition despite the passing of time and where the Irish language is very much alive. Holdings are small and although life has been made a lot easier in the past decades by the availability of special aid grants from the EC and the Irish government, many families are large and emigration is widespread.

Attempts to preserve the Irish language are bolstered by Radio na Gaeltacht and Irish summer colleges where students come from all over the country to speak their native tongue, learn Ceili dancing and stay in the houses of Irish-speaking families.

Most travellers who have written about Galway agree that it possesses in abundance two attributes: atmosphere and character. Sean O'Faolain, the famous novelist once wrote: "No man who wants his daughter to learn the truth about life could do better than send her for six months to Galway where they will tell you story after story in gushing delight... yet I think my daughter might well return from Galway and say to me in an awed voice, 'Father, is that the truth?' I should have to say, 'My child, of course it is not the truth. But it is life!'"

RESTAURANTS & PUBS

**MCSWIGGANS
RESTAURANT AND PUB
3 EYRE STREET, WOOD QUAY
GALWAY**
Tel: (091) 68917
Fax: (091) 61513

McSwiggans restaurant and pub is located just off Eyre Square on Eyre Street in Galway city. The pub is a marvellous example of the classic traditional Irish pub. Upstairs there is an excellent restaurant offering a varied menu at very reasonable prices.

**DUN AONGHASA RESTAURANT
KILRONAN
ARAN ISLANDS
CO. GALWAY**

If you gravitate toward traditional settings you'll love this wood-and-stone family restaurant, with its cosy open fire. Overlooking Galway Bay it specialises in the freshest of local seafood and home baking.
Seats groups of 90 persons.

Full drinks license including comprehensive wine list. Specialises in location lobster picnics.
Information – Bookings:
Phone/Fax P.-J. or Grace
(099) 61104

Raftery's Rest
**AWARD WINNING
BAR & RESTAURANT
KILCOLGAN
CO GALWAY**
Tel: (091) 96175
Fax: (091) 96038

Specialist in seafood, oysters and clams. Extensive bar food menu served all day, 7 days. Entertainment every Saturday night, traditional music every Sunday night. Owner/Manager: Terry Wilson. Located 9 miles from Galway on main Galway—Limerick road.

VISITS & ACTIVITIES

GALWAY CULTURAL INSTITUTE
Come learn English in the beautiful surroundings of Galway!
THE PLACE!
Galway is a beautiful city on the edge of Connemara and the Burren. It is the perfect place to learn English. It is easy to meet people and talk to them.
THE REASON!
Programmes are tailor made to the individual learner's needs and learning style.
THE METHOD!
Communicative/Functional training taught by highly qualified staff.
THE COURSES!
English for General Use, English for Specific Purposes, Academic English, Short Intensive Courses and programmes for Juniors that include activities, Preparation for Cambridge Examinations.
For further information contact:
Celestine Rowland
Galway Cultural Institute,
84 Clybaun Heights, Salthill, Galway, Ireland. Tel: 353-91-23550/28511
Fax: 353-91-65548/23550

**KYLEMORE ABBEY
CRAFT SHOP / RESTAURANT
KYLEMORE ABBEY, CONNEMARA
CO GALWAY**
Tel: (095) 41113 / 41146
A Benedictine Abbey of unsurpassed splendour situated in the silent hills of Connemara. The Nuns invite visitors to the Abbey (part of), the grounds, pottery and extensive craft shops featuring quality Irish products - fashion ware, handknits, linens, books, jewellery, including their exclusive range of crystal and pottery, and to sample the best of cookery from home-grown produce. Open Easter to October.

ACCOMMODATION

**BRENNANS YARD HOTEL
LOWER MERCHANTS ROAD
GALWAY**
Tel: (091) 68166
Fax: (091) 68262
Located in the heart of Galway city, Brennans Yard is a charming, intimate hotel with excellent standards of accommodation, food and service. Our en suite bedrooms have been individually designed

and are furnished with pine furniture. In our restaurant, you can dine in discreet elegance. The Oyster Bar offers a mouthwatering range of traditional seafood dishes. The unique atrium height conservatory and original works of art all contribute to the warmth and individuality of Brennans Yard.

WHERE TO SHOP

**HARTMANN JEWELLERS
29 WILLIAM STREET
GALWAY**
Tel: (091) 62063
Fax: (091) 62010
Hartmanns are the West of Ireland's leading jewellers. They carry an exquisite range of 18ct gold, diamond and precious gem set jewellery and are also the agents for many watches of distinction including – **Rolex, Omega, Tag Heuer, Gucci, Longines and Swatch**.
Galway is the home of the famous claddagh ring and Hartmanns are Galway's specialist Claddagh Jewellers. Each ring is handcrafted on the premises by skilled jewellers in 9, 14 and 18 carat gold in a range of styles and sizes to suit individual tastes.

**ROYAL TARA CHINA
TARA HALL, MERVUE
GALWAY**
Phone: (091) 51301
Fax: (091) 57574
Royal Tara China offers a complimentary factory tour, where you can witness the creation of their many handcrafted collections.
For that perfect gift, browse through the showrooms, which houses handpainted Irish birds, cottages, figurines and superb handpainted china tableware and giftware.
Facilities also include Restaurant, Bureau de change, Cashback and Mail order.
Factory shop open 7 days 9-6 all year.

COUNTY KILDARE

Lying close to Dublin this is one of the most prosperous and populated counties. Kildare is the centre of Ireland's bloodstock industry. The county is divided by the River Liffey on the north east and the basin of the Barrow in the south.

The Grand Canal crosses the countryside linking Dublin with the River Shannon at Banagher. The canal was built in the 1760's and carried agricultural produce between Dublin and the River Barrow at Athy. The railways destroyed the canal's passenger and commercial trade, but today the Grand Canal has been restored. The canalside has some very attractive walks and is also excellent for coarse fishing and canoeing.

Because of Kildare's proximity to Dublin, many people choose to live in its peaceful countryside and commute to work in the city.

Kildare Town is an important horse breeding centre with the National Stud at Tully nearby. A 10th century round tower and the remains of an important monastic site are situated in the centre of the town. St Brigid founded a nunnery here in the 6th century although by the 7th century it had become a monastery. Legend tells how St Brigid, when she asked the ruling king to grant her land to build her nunnery, was told by him that he would give only what her cloak would cover. Brigid dropped her cloak and it grew and grew to many acres and the king could do nothing but grant her the land.

On the edge of Kildare is the Curragh, a limestone plain that stretches for kilometres in the direction of Dublin. The land is said to be good because the pasture that grows is the best in the world for building bone. But it is the skill of the local breeders in choosing the sires that has made Curragh bloodstock so successful. The Curragh Races is an experience not to be missed. The skills of the trainers, jockeys and horses are put to the test whilst the punters down the Guinness with the conversation neverending. The atmosphere is electric as the horses thunder along on the superb green course. The most famous of the Curragh meetings are the Irish Sweeps Derby, the Irish 2000 Guineas, the Irish Oaks and the St Leger. Another famous race course not far from the Curragh is Punchestown, near Naas, the county's administrative centre.

Kildare is also a county full of folklore. The Hill of Allen (206m) is famous as the other world seat of the great Celtic warrior, Fionn MacCumhaill. The Hill, together with Naas and Knockaulin, was a residence of the kings of Leinster. The Rath of Mullaghmast near Ballitore is an earthen stone fort full of legends. It is said that the 11th Earl of Kildare, Garret Og Fitzgerald, sleeps here emerging once every seven years!

County Kildare is also an important seat of learning. Maynooth has one of the country's most highly regarded universities. It is also famous for St Patrick's College, one of the greatest Catholic seminaries in the world. The college's ecclesiastical museum includes vestments made by Marie Antoinette for an Irish chaplain.

109

KILDARE
Population: 122,516
Land Area: 654 sq.miles/
1693 sq.km

NAAS:
Population:11,140
Distance from:
Dublin - 21 miles/34km
Cork - 137 miles/220 km
Shannon - 111 miles/178km
Rosslare - 98 miles/158km

Rail Service: Dublin/Cork -
Kildare

Airport: None

Tourist Office:
Newbridge
Tel: 045 33835
Open June - Aug.

VISITS & ACTIVITIES

CASTLETOWN HOUSE
CELBRIDGE, CO KILDARE
Tel: (01) 628 8252
Fax: (01) 627 1811

Ireland's largest and finest Palladian country house, begun c. 1722 for William Conolly, Speaker of Irish House of Commons. Designed by Italian architect, Alessandro Galilei, also in part by Irish architect, Sir Edward Lovett Pearce. Famous state rooms contain collection of 18th century furniture and painting. Coffee Shop and Restaurant. 13 miles from Dublin, open throughout the year, every day Apr.-Sept.

IRISH NATIONAL STUD
JAPANESE GARDENS
TULLY
KILDARE, CO KILDARE
Tel: (045) 21617
Fax: (045) 22129

The Japanese Gardens, created 1906-1910, renowned as the finest in Europe, symbolise the "Life of Man".
Open from EASTER - OCTOBER, guided tours for groups (20+) available on request.
Visitors can also include a visit to the National Stud and Horse Museum at the same entry point as the Gardens.

COUNTY KERRY

KERRY
Population: 124,159
Land Area: 1833 sq. miles/
4745 sq. km

TRALEE:
Population:17,109
Distance from:
Dublin - 188 miles/302 km
Cork - 75 miles/121 km
Shannon - 80 miles/129 km
Rosslare - 181 miles/291km

Rail Service:
Dublin - Killarney/Tralee
Cork - Killarney/Tralee

Airport:
Farranfore International Airport
15 km from Tralee
21 km from Killarney
Tel: 066 64350

Tourist Office:
Killarney
Tel: 064 31633
Open All Year
Tralee
Tel: 066 21288
Open All Year

Kerry is packed with some of the country's most beautiful scenery, friendliest people and liveliest legends. It boasts the opulent lakes of Killarney and an expansive National Park with the beautiful Muckross House and Gardens at its centre, set amongst the highest mountain range in the country, the Macgillycuddy Reeks.

To the west are the breathtaking peninsulas of Dingle and Iveragh (more commonly known as the Ring of Kerry). Here the rugged mountains sweep down to an often savage Atlantic ocean. Lying off the coast are some interesting islands. The Skelligs rise dramatically from the sea and lie at the mouth of Ballinskelligs Bay. The small Skellig is covered in thousands of gannets, whilst the greater Skellig or Skellig Michael, has an almost perfect example of an early monastic settlement. By comparison with the Skelligs, the island of Valentia, lying just west off Cahirciveen, has softer scenery. It was the European terminal of the first trans-Atlantic cable laid in August 1857. The cable played an important role in strengthening the area's already strong links with America. Indeed it is said that during the early part of the 19thC this part of Kerry was so cut off from the rest of the country that it had greater contacts with America than with Dublin and that newspapers and letters from the capital arrived via New York!

This county, like so many along the western seaboard, suffered constantly from unemployment and emigration and that even today its people tend to look west across the Atlantic rather than east across the hills for their trade and human contact. Perhaps this has helped to create a psychological distance which appears to make Kerry and its people somehow different. Kerry folk make their living off small farm holdings, by fishing and more importantly by tourism. Killarney is the most developed tourist centre in Ireland. It offers lively night life along with the possibility to escape into the wild and unspoilt countryside within minutes. One of the best ways to explore the area around Killarney is by pony and trap in the company of a wise and jovial jarvey. All jarveys have tales to tell and stories to spin. Like all Kerry folk they are quick-witted with a droll sense of humour. One wonders therefore how such folk have become the butt of 'stupid' jokes made by other Irish people. Thus: How do you recognise a Kerryman in a hospital if his wife has given birth to twins? - He's the one that has spent a week running around trying to find the father of the second baby!

Kerrymen can be proud however that their county produced one of the greatest Irish leaders, Daniel O'Connell who, in 1829, won Catholic emancipation. Apart from the enigmatic figure of O'Connell, the county is steeped in history and legend going right back to the Bronze Age. Kerry beaches were the landing places for many of the invasions, voyages and battles of the past. The beach at Waterville on the Ring of Kerry is very beautiful and palm trees and wild fuschia imbue it with a continental air. It was near here that according to local stories, Cessair, the granddaughter of Noah, landed with her father, two other men and 49 women. They were hoping to escape the Great Flood of the Bible. Apparently the year was 2958 BC! The women divided the three men between them. Two of the men died and the third, Fintan, was so reluctant to remain with the women that he fled. He later turned himself into a salmon!

Off the dramatic corniche, at Slea Head on the Dingle Peninsula, lie the Blasket Islands. They have been uninhabited since 1953 when the young emigrated because of the harsh living conditions. It was from this Gaelic speaking area of Kerry that some of the most beautiful Irish writing sprung in the past. The accounts of island life left through the writing records the warmth and the fun as well as the misery and the heartbreak experienced by the islanders. The impressive biography "The Island Man" has been translated into various different languages.

Kerry is not only famous for its bee-hive huts, ogham stones, stone forts and incredible beauty. It is also famous for its festivals. During the first week of September each year, young women with Irish roots come from all over the world to partake in the now famous Rose of Tralee festival. Whilst the Rose is being chosen, Tralee and half of Ireland have one big party!

NOTE: For quick and direct access to Co Clare, take the Tarbert/Killimer car ferry accross the Shannon Estuary.

ACCOMMODATION

MUCKROSS PARK HOTEL
LAKES OF KILLARNEY
CO KERRY
Tel: (064) 31938
Fax: (064) 31965

The Muckross Park Hotel is a redevelopment of the oldest hotel in Killarney. Welcoming visitors since 1795, the hotel retains the luxurious feel of a traditional Irish country house but with the comfort and convenience of modern facilities and 4* service. The 25 guest rooms are exceptional by any standard and both of our suites are simply unique.
Located on the border of Killarney National Park and the Bourne-Vincent estate, with Killarney Lakes only minutes walk away, the Muckross Park Hotel is an ideal venue for a relaxing holiday.

WHERE TO SHOP

CLEO IRELAND LTD
2 SHELBOURNE STREET
KENMARE, CO KERRY
Open April-November
Tel: (064) 41410
Also: 18 Kildare Street
Dublin 2
Open all year.
Tel: (01) 761421

Retail and wholesale. Cleo's is a family business, established 1936. We design our own clothing using themes from Ireland's past, in natural fabrics specially chosen and woven for us from pure wool and linen, in colours of the Irish countryside.

VISITS & ACTIVITIES

MUCKROSS HOUSE AND
GARDENS
KILLARNEY, CO KERRY
Enquiries: Tel: (064) 31440
Fax: (064) 33926

* Beautiful furnished Elizabethan-style mansion, now the centre of Kerry folk life and history.
* Skilled craftworkers using traditional methods produce high quality items of weaving, pottery and bookbinding.
* Free audio-visual introduction.
* World renowned gardens.
* Nature trails, scenic walks and views.
* Stables, craftshop and "coach house restaurant".
OPEN DAILY ALL YEAR ROUND.

HORSE DRAWN GYPSY
CARAVANS
Telex: 73123
Phone: (066) 26277
Fax: (066) 25981.

Hire a beautiful Irish horse and a fully-equipped Gypsy Caravan and go roaming the rainbows of Ireland laden with nothing but freedom. Each caravan can sleep up to 5 persons and is equipped with blankets, cooking utensils and gas stove. The season is April through October. A week is recommended : short breaks also available.
Price from £250 per week for the horse and caravan. Instructions and maps included. Located in Co Kerry in the south west corner of Ireland. Brochure: Slattery's Travel, 1 Russell Street, Tralee, Co Kerry, Ireland.

RESTAURANTS & PUBS

THE ISLANDMAN
MAIN STREET
DINGLE, CO KERRY
Tel: (065) 51803

The Islandman is a most unique restaurant that combines a bookshop and bar. The restaurant specializes in the very best of fresh local produce.
Fish, meat and vegetarian dishes, the Islandman is open all the time. A fine range of books of Irish interest, plus loads of good novels make the Islandman definitely a place not to be missed when you come to Dingle.

O'CONNOR'S ABBEY TAVERN
ABBEYDORNEY
NEAR TRALEE
CO KERRY (ON ROUTE TO
TARBERT CAR FERRY)
Tel: (066) 35145

Old time country village pub offering Irish hospitality, home-cooked snacks and meals. Situated in idyllic setting, convenient to Killarney, Dingle, Ring of Kerry, 5 miles from sandy beaches. Golf: Tralee and Ballybunion. Fishing and horse riding nearby. Traditional Irish music. Children welcome. An experience not to be missed!

THE ARMADA RESTAURANT &
AN REALT BAR
STRAND STREET
DINGLE, CO KERRY
Tel: (066) 51505
Fax: (066) 51478

Long established family-run, fully licensed restaurant and bar specialising in distinctive food prepared from the superb produce of local waters and pastures. Fresh Atlantic salmon, seatrout, crab etc, daily. Situated overlooking Dingle Pier. Open hearth fires and traditional music nightly. Beidh céad míle fáilte romhat! from your hosts Mark and Anne Kerry.

THE HUNTSMAN
WATERVILLE, CO KERRY
Tel: (0667) 4124
Fax: (0667) 4560

Award-winning gourmet restaurant situated on seafront as you approach Waterville village. Specialising in the freshest of fine seafood. Also a range of meats, poultry, pasta and vegetarian dishes to suit all tastes and appetites. Extensive selection of wines – award winning wine list (Grahams Port).
Recommended by all major good food guides. Warm and friendly atmosphere with magnificent views of Ballinskellig Bay. We also offer first class accommodation en suite on beachfront. Your hosts Raymond and Deirdre welcome you.

Ireland

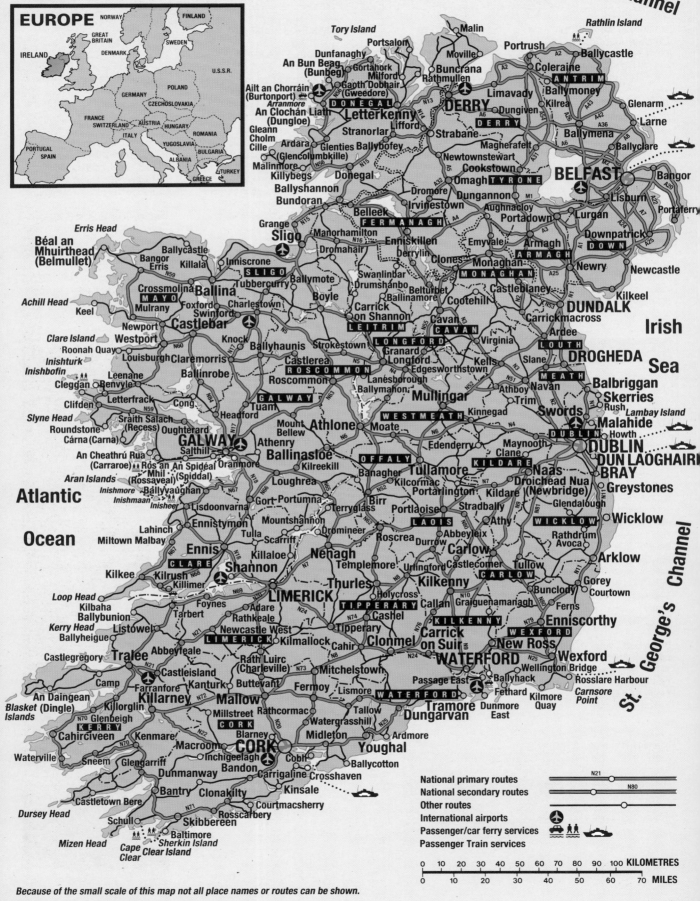

Map legend:

National primary routes
National secondary routes
Other routes
International airports
Passenger/car ferry services
Passenger Train services

0 10 20 30 40 50 60 70 80 90 100 **KILOMETRES**

0 10 20 30 40 50 60 70 **MILES**

Because of the small scale of this map not all place names or routes can be shown.

Cartography: Tony Meighan Ltd.

COUNTY OFFALY

Offaly was described in a 19th century guide book as "the county you travel through on your way from Dublin to the south-west". That doesn't exactly sound very exciting, but it refers to a long tradition of this area being a major 'traffic junction' in Ireland which even in early times, when travelling was difficult and dangerous, saw many travellers come and go. The main routes of the time are not easy to see for the modern-day traveller who stays on the main road. But the old routes always led along the water-ways or any line of hills where you had a good view of the – then wooded - plains. A closer look will show both in this area – the mighty Shannon, longest river in the British Isles, which flows through Ireland in a north-south direction, and the Eiscir Riada, a long winding gravel ridge left by retreating glaciers after the last ice age. At the crossing of these two main ancient travel routes we can today find one of the most important centres of Irish religious life – Clonmacnois. This ancient monastry was founded in 545 A.D. by St. Ciaran and, although in ruins for centuries, still show the typical ground plan of many such sites in Ireland. Unlike the compact and ordered plan of the monasteries that were later introduced from the continent, buildings here are scattered over quite a large area. There are two round-towers, a number of small churches and three impressive Irish high crosses.

Today another type of pilgrim visits this county, nature-lovers come here to see the wetlands around the river Shannon, the meadows full of flowers, and especially the large areas of bog which for so many visitors form an integral part of their picture of Ireland. Bord na Mona, the semi-state body in charge of managing and exploiting large areas of bogland here, offers an interesting information tour across the bog by train which gives you an insight into the formation and many uses of turf. If you want to experience untouched bogs and happen to have your wellingtons with you, a walk through Clara Bog or the Slieve Bloom Environment Park might be an idea, the latter is well signposted and also suitable for walkers who have no experience with bogland. If after your trip through this unspoilt landscape you are quite happy to return to the civilized world, Birr town is where you should go. This small town seems not to have changed much in the last century, the neatly laid out squares and streets, the well-kept Georgian houses and, above all, Birr Castle with its large surrounding park make Birr a very special country town which is definitely worth a visit.

Offaly is a truly idyllic part of Ireland, cosmopolitan enough to be able to welcome its visitors with all modern comforts, and yet remote enough to make them enjoy the undisturbed peace and tranquility which for so many is such an important part of this country.

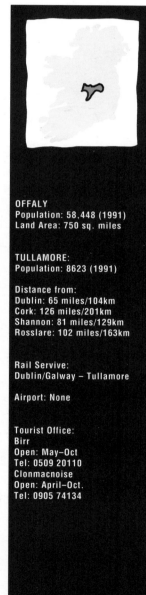

113

ACCOMMODATION

COUNTY ARMS HOTEL
BIRR
CO. OFFALY
Tel: (0509) 20791
Fax: (0509) 21234

Superb Georgian residence built in 1810 and recently transformed into a comfortable and relatively inexpensive in-town hotel, which comprises all rooms en-suite. We pride ourselves on our exceptional cuisine, with much fresh produce emanating from our large and well maintained hotel garden and greenhouse.
Being in the heart of Ireland with lakes, mountains, marshland and rivers and at least 8 Golf Courses within reasonable proximity, our hotel is the ideal base for golfing, fishing, shooting and outdoor pursuits enthusiasts.

BROSNA LODGE HOTEL
BANAGHER
CO. OFFALY
Tel: (0509) 51350
Fax: (0509) 51521
Our country house hotel close to the banks of the river Shannon, welcomes guests with superb hospitality and relaxed elegancy.

Its recently refurbished bedrooms, all en-suite, complement the exquisite food and service in Snipes Restaurant. Serene mature gardens surround the hotel. With unique peat bogs, mountains, the river Shannon and Clonmacnoise you will delight in this gentle and little known part of Ireland. Fishing, golf, trekking, nature and historical tours can be arranged locally. Brosna Lodge Hotel in Banagher. A beautiful place to stay.

VISITS & ACTIVITIES

CHARLEVILLE FOREST CASTLE
TULLAMORE, CO OFFALY
Tel: (0506) 21279
Fax: (0506) 21279

Charleville Forest Castle was designed in 1798 by Ireland's legendary architect, Francis Johnstone. It was the original of the neo-gothic buildings, and its very fine limestone exterior and magnificent plasterwork interior are among the most beautiful in the country. It is called "The Fairy Tale Castle". Charleville is located in an ancient forest in the Heart of Ireland where stands the eight hundred year old oak called "The King Tree".

BIRR CASTLE DEMESNE
BIRR
CO. OFFALY
Tel/Fax: (0509) 20056

Don't miss the world's largest telescope from the last century and box hedges from the century before, our special Expo '93 on castle cooking called "Sugar and Spice ..." and much, much more in the award-winning and double starred
BIRR CASTLE DEMESNE
now open every day of the year

🅿 🏨 🏠 ☕ ✕ ℹ £-$

CLONMACNOISE & WEST OFFALY RAILWAY
The only one of its kind in Europe.

A unique opportunity to enjoy an 8 km guided rail journey on a circular route in a luxury train coach which gives an insight into an internationally raised bog in Co. Offaly.
The landscape is like a book which tells its own fantastic story – once you learn how to read the language in which it is written. Regular schedule – Easter to Oct. on the hour 10 a.m. to 5 p.m.
GROUP BOOKINGS – ALL YEAR ROUND (0905) 74114, 74172, 74121

OFFALY
Population: 58,448 (1991)
Land Area: 750 sq. miles

TULLAMORE:
Population: 8623 (1991)

Distance from:
Dublin: 65 miles/104km
Cork: 126 miles/201km
Shannon: 81 miles/129km
Rosslare: 102 miles/163km

Rail Servive:
Dublin/Galway – Tullamore

Airport: None

Tourist Office:
Birr
Open: May–Oct
Tel: 0509 20110
Clonmacnoise
Open: April–Oct.
Tel: 0905 74134

COUNTY MAYO/SLIGO

MAYO
Population:115,184
Land Area: 2157 sq. miles/
5584 sq.km

CASTLEBAR
Population: 6,349
Distance from:
Dublin - 146 miles/235 km
Cork - 191 miles/307 km
Shannon - 120 miles/193 km
Rosslare - 211 miles/339 km

Rail Service:
Dublin - Castlebar/Westport
Airport:
Knock International Airport
7km from Charlestown
Tel: 094 67222

Tourist Office:
Westport
Tel: 098 25711 Open All Year.

SLIGO
Population: 56,046
Land Area: 709 sq. miles
1835 sq.km

SLIGO TOWN:
Population: 17,259
Distance from:
Dublin - 133 miles/214km
Cork - 208 miles/335 km
Shannon - 136 miles/219 km
Rosslare - 198 miles/319 km

Rail Service:
Dublin - Sligo
Airport:
Sligo Airport
8 km from town centre
Tel: 071 68280

Tourist Office:
Aras Reddan, Sligo
Tel: 071 61201 Open All Year

Mayo may be a county of poor land which has lost many of its sons to far off shores, but it has some of the most spectacular and lonely scenery in the west of Ireland. Quartzite, schist and gneiss form dramatic mountains and cliffs and the Atlantic is a wonderful backdrop for the fuschia covered inlets, the sandy beaches, the soft green hills and the wild and heathery bogs. Besides farming, the county has traditionally provided employment through localised industries such as Foxford Woollen Mills in Foxford. In recent times the region has gained considerable employment through the setting up of industries by foreign companies in such centres as Ballina, Castlebar, Claremorris and Westport.

Ireland's third largest county has a long tradition of forced emigration and as a result has developed links with the USA in particular. Some of her sons have done well for themselves in their adopted countries and villages like Bohola can boast of having numerous dollar millionaires as sons. These sons were compelled to leave because traditional family holdings were small and under the system primo genito, the responsibility of the land was left to the eldest son. Thousands emigrated during the post war years leaving behind one of the most depopulated parts of the country. Mayo's population had already suffered during the great famine years when it diminished to less than 50% as thousands died from starvation and others fled on the coffin ships bound for such ports as Boston and New York.

Nowadays, tourism plays a vital and important role in improving the county's economy and lessening the numbers who emigrate. The most important tourist centre in Mayo is the place of pilgrimage called Knock. It was here in 1879 that the Virgin Mary, St Joseph and St John appeared to 14 people. Although it rained heavily on the witnesses, the area around the apparition remained dry. It was to celebrate the shrine's centenary that the Pope visited Knock in 1979 at the request of the then parish priest, Mons. James Horan. Mons Horan was a dynamic character who persuaded big business companies and the government that this part of the country needed an international airport. In what became a political football and was regarded as one big joke at the time, Mons Horan persisted and built his runway. One local story recalls how when first built, the runway was used by local motorists as a type of race track as it was the only piece of straight road in the whole of the country! Horan International Airport was opened in 1986 and now has regular flights to the UK and Europe and has certainly turned the charming and vibrant town of Westport into a growing attraction for visitors from Ireland and abroad..

To the south-west of Knock is Clew Bay where one finds Ireland's sacred mountain, Croagh Patrick. This is where St Patrick is believed to have spent 40 days and nights fasting and in prayer. From the summit he also, according to legend, rang a bell and banished all snakes from the Emerald Isle! The fact that there are no snakes in Ireland is most probably as a result of the last Ice Age. The mountain which is made of quartzite breaks up into sharp-edged stones and is not very comfortable for climbing. Nevertheless thousands of pilgrims climb it bare foot every July. The summit affords one of the finest panoramic views in Ireland.

The English writer, William Thackeray who visited the west in 1842, described the scenery around Clew Bay as the 'most beautiful in the world'.

Mayo is steeped in history and legend and this part of the coast and the islands off it are associated with a warrior woman, Granuaile, otherwise known as Grace O'Malley. She outshone all her male contemporaries in the qualities of leadership. She was a pirate captain and her symbol was the seahorse. Her family had been lords of the isles for two hundred years and in the 40 years it took the Tudors to extend their power in Ireland, Granuaile was the mainstay of the rebellion in the west. One of the stories which seem to explain her best is as follows. At the age of 45 she gave birth at sea to her first child, Toby. An hour later her ship was boarded by Turkish pirates. The battle on the deck was almost lost, when she appeared wrapped in a blanket and shot the enemy captain with a blunderbuss. After that her men rallied, captured the Turkish ship and hanged the crew. Her story is documented in an interpretive exhibition on permanent display in Louisburg.

Co Mayo's unique landscape, the welcoming attitude of its people and its many varied visitor attractions has led to increased attention by Irish and foreign tourists over the past two to three years.

Sligo's beauty has been immortilized in the poetic works of Nobel Prize winner, W B Yeats and in the paintings of his brother Jack B Yeats. Physically, Sligo has a lot in common with neighbouring Mayo - steep cliffs, wide loughs and only a handful of towns and villages to interrupt the beautiful countryside. This country contains everything necessary for a major tourist centre yet Sligo is one of the least discovered of the western seaboard counties.

Its beautiful lakes, such as Lough Gill, rival those of Killarney. It has long golden beaches, dramatic mountains, numerous archaeological sites and is steeped in folklore. Although tourism is not as developed as in other areas it is rapidly becoming an important element in the creation of employment. Sligo now boasts its own flourishing regional airport.

ACCOMMODATION

BREAFFY HOUSE HOTEL
CASTLEBAR
CO MAYO
Tel: (094) 22033
Fax: (094) 22033

Breaffy House Hotel is a Grade A Manor House Hotel set in 60 acres of rolling parkland, just two miles from Castlebar, the capital of Mayo. The friendly and professional staff will make sure your stay, short or long, is relaxed and comfortable. All bedrooms offer ensuite facilities, TV, radio, direct dial telephones and tea/coffee making facilities. Our restaurant is renowned locally for its fine foods and wines. We are the ideal location for exploring the west of Ireland.

WHERE TO SHOP

ASH-LING CRAFTS
THE OCTAGON
WESTPORT, CO MAYO
Tel: (098) 25376   Fax: (098) 26014

When you come to this beautiful town with its tree lined malls and unique atmosphere, come and see our selection of Irish gifts for the discerning customer. We offer knitwear, craftwork, jewellery, music, film, bureau de change and stamps. Open 7 days a week in high season. We at Ash-Ling Crafts wish you an enjoyable stay when you come to the west of Ireland.

FOXFORD WOOLLEN MILLS (EST. 1892)
FOXFORD, CO MAYO
Tel: (091) 56104

Imagine a unique and thriving woollen mills, set in wild and rugged West of Ireland. Famous for its tweeds, rugs and blankets. Established in 1892 by a woman before her time. One nun's vision has become our reality at Foxford Woollen Mills and Visitors' Centre, Foxford, Co Mayo. Come and relive her story of success against incredible odds. Take the industrial tour. Experience the sights, sounds and smells of this 19th century woollen mills. Relax in our comfortable restaurant. Browse through our impressive mill shop.
Opening hours: Mon - Sat: 10am - 6pm. Sun: 2pm -6pm.
FOXFORD - A LEGEND IN QUALITY.

HACKETT & TURPIN
CARROWTEIGE
BELMULLET, CO MAYO
Tel: (097) 88925
Fax: (097) 88924

Hackett & Turpin make Ireland's finest hand-loomed sweaters in silk, wool, cotton and linen/cotton. Their famous hand-looming skills are cleverly used to produce refined, modern sweaters in luxury natural fibres. Hackett & Turpin sweaters are available in specially selected stores throughout Ireland.

Visitors are also welcome to view the skills of the Hackett & Turpin workers at the factory in Carrowteige, Belmullet, North Mayo. Telephone (097) 88925.

VISITS & ACTIVITIES

OUR LADY'S SHRINE
KNOCK, CO MAYO
Enquiries: Tel: (094) 88100
Fax: (094) 88295

- National Marian Shrine
- Programme 25th April to 10th October 1993
- 7 public Masses daily
- Public Devotions 2.15pm
- Confessions 11.00am - 6.00pm
- Knock Folk Museum. Open daily 10.00am - 18.00pm
- Knock Caravan and Camping Park. Tourers welcome. Mobile homes for hire.

ACHILL ISLAND TOURISM COMMITTEE
KEEL, ACHILL
CO MAYO
Tel: (098) 43123

Achill. It's far west. Out on the Atlantic. Storms, surf, sun keep it clean. It's an island. You drive on. It's self-contained. Fifteen miles around. It's not bleak. It's alive in sudden mountains, bogs, water always changing colour. Everything's in proportion. Turn every corner, there's magic before you, and beaches, blue flags brightly waving. And donkeys wait for you. It's gorgeous. It's Achill.

COUNTY WATERFORD/WEXFORD

WATERFORD
Population: 91,151 (1986)
Land Area: 709 sq.miles/
1835 sq. km

WATERFORD CITY:
Population: 39,529
Distance from:
Dublin - 97 miles/156 km
Cork - 78 miles/126 km
Shannon - 95 miles/153 km
Rosslare - 50 miles/80 km

Rail Service:
Dublin - Waterford
Rosslare - Waterford
Airport: Waterford Airport
10 km from city centre
Tel: 051 75580

Tourist Office:
Waterford City
Tel: 051 75788 Open All Year.

WEXFORD
Population: 102,552 (1986)
Land Area: 908 sq. miles/
2350 sq.km

WEXFORD TOWN:
Population: 10,336
Distance from:
Dubin - 87 miles/140 km
Cork - 117 miles/18 km
Shannon - 133 miles/214 km
Rosslare - 12 miles/19 km

Rail Service:
Dublin - Wexford
Rosslare - Wexford
Airport: None

Tourist Office:
Wexford Town
053 23111 Open All Year
Rosslare Ferry Terminal
053 33622 Open All Year

Waterford is in the sunny southeast which has a reputation for being the warmest and driest area of the country. This is a county of fertile farmland with rolling green pastures, rugged mountain beauty and an Atlantic coastline dotted with small fishing villages, beaches and holiday resorts. Waterford City lies in a valley drained by the river Suir, which flows into the river Nore, which in turn flows in the river Barrow. In the mythological account of pre-history Ireland, "The Book of Invasions", the first Celts described the site as a "sweet confluence of waters, a trinity of rivers". The city, which lies on the south bank of the Suir, has a proud history. The Vikings founded the city in AD850 and used it as a base for raids up the rivers to the rich valleys of Tipperary and beyond. In the past the city had strong connections with continental Europe and some of these connections are maintained through its busy container port and its world famous glass factory. The city has a reputation for good pubs and wine bars and the old parts of the city are quite attractive. In September the local Theatre Royal hosts the Waterford International Festival of Light Opera. In an ideal position for visitors coming by ferry from Britain and the continent Waterford has a growing tourist industry. Some of its pretty coastal villages are important holiday resorts for Irish people. Tramore has a beach which stretches for 5km and with the warm Gulf Stream it is ideal for bathers and windsurfers. Nearby is the remarkable Knockeen dolmen which dates back to 5000BC and probably marks the grave of a pre-celtic Desai chieftain.

Wexford, like Waterford, is a county of rich farmland with low rolling hills and fertile valleys. With a warm climate and light sandy beaches and it is a favourite place for Irish holidaymakers. Tower houses dating from the 14th century are a common feature along with many well maintained thatched cottages. Rosslare is a major ferryport with services to France and to Britain. Wexford's proximity to Britain and the continent has played a part in its history. It was here that the Norman invasion took place. Wexford was also the ancestral home of the late president of the USA, John F Kennedy. The Kennedy homestead is at Duganstown near New Ross and nearby is the John F Kennedy Memorial Park, a major tourist attraction. Wexford Town is internationally famous for its Opera Festival. Held annually in October, this week of first class music and performances specialises in rarely produced works. Wexford Town is full of character with its narrow streets, quaint pubs and lively coloured houses. To Irish people county Wexford is historically associated with the 1798 insurrection against British rule. Thousands of peasants armed with pitchforks held off the well trained forces of the English for six weeks until they were defeated at Vinegar Hill with huge losses. Enniscorthy, which is situated near Vinegar Hill is an attractive market town on the river Slaney. In the west of the county are the Blackstairs Mountains where one can sometimes spot wild deer. The small sheep farms on the slopes of the mountains are in great contrast to prosperous larger farms in the rest of the county.

ACCOMMODATION

BLACKWATER LODGE HOTEL
UPPER BALLYDUFF
WATERFORD
Tel: (058) 60235
Fax: (058) 60162

Overlooking the unspoilt Blackwater Valley and River. Cosy family-run hotel specialising in fishing (30 miles salmon/trout/seatrout rivers) and hunting (deer and duck) with tackle shop, smokery and ghillies, but where the whole family can relax and enjoy the amenities in the valley and nearby coast. Fully licensed with a la carte restaurant. Ample golf, equestrian and sports facilities in the area.

RESTAURANTS & PUBS

THE STRAND HOTEL
DUNMORE EAST
CO WATERFORD
Tel: (051) 83174

The Strand is a small friendly family owned restaurant and pub. It sits on a sandy beach opposite the harbour. The food is good, fresh and without pretensions, using only the best of Irish ingredients - the fresh fish are landed daily in the harbour, locally grown vegetables and herbs, great steaks, homemade desserts and ice cream - all combine to make the Strand, Dunmore East, a place well worth a detour. Open 7 days from Easter. Lunch 1pm-2.30pm. Dinner 7pm-10pm. Visa, Access, Diners.

GALLEY CRUISING RESTAURANT
NEW ROSS
CO WEXFORD AND WATERFORD
Tel: (051) 21723
Minitel: (051) 21950

On your route from Rosslare Harbour, enjoy a scenic river cruise and delicious meal, all prepared by our own chefs from fresh local produce. Inclusive price lunch £11, 12.30h. Afternoon tea £5, 15.00h. Dinner 18.00 or 19.00, £17 to £20. April/November. Heated saloons. Fully licensed. "The best of Irish tourism".

STEP BACK THROUGH TIME..

and experience the uniqueness of Ireland's Past.

THE IRISH NATIONAL HERITAGE PARK.
Ferrycarrig, Wexford. Tel: (053)-41733/22211/23111. Fax: 23406
"A unique outdoor museum demonstrating the life of Ireland from 9000 years ago"
Walk through 12 hectares of beautiful countryside with streams, ponds and wildlife.
14 separate sites showing the homesteads and lifestyles of Ireland from 7000 B.C.
- Celtic Fortifications, Viking Boats and Norman Castles - Many hands - on and
working displays. Magnificent views of the River Slaney and its Estuary.
Walk the park and understand the make-up of Ireland with its Celtic,
Viking and Norman influences. Audio Visual presentation, guided
tours, souvenir and coffee shop, picnic areas and children's
playground all available on site.

CELTWORLD
Tramore, Co. Waterford.
Tel: (051) 86166.
Fax: (051) 90146
Experience excitement, magic and
mystery and take a fasinating journey
through time to where legend lives.. The myths
and legends that are so much a part of Ireland's
Celtic past are now being brought to life at Celtworld
where astonishing technology recaptures the spirit of
Ireland in this magical era.

LISMORE HERITAGE TOWN
& VISITOR CENTRE
Lismore, Co. Waterford.
Tel: (058) 54975   Fax: (058) 53009
Visit the "Lismore Experience" an award winning multi-media
presentation in which your host Brother Declan (alias Niall Tóibín)
takes you on an enthralling journey through time, starting with the
arrival of St. Carthage in 636 and bringing you right up to the present.
Today's urban settlement of Lismore is located in one of the prettiest settings
in Ireland and is charmingly decorated with a fine collection of 18th and 19th
century buildings. The "Lismore Experience" is an ideal point of departure from
which to explore the ancient treasures of the town and its surrounding countryside.

118

WICKLOW
Population: 94,542 (1986)
Land Area: 781 sq.miles/
2022 sq.km

WICKLOW TOWN:
Population: 5,304
Distance from:
Dublin - 32 miles/51 km
Cork - 164 miles/264 km
Shannon - 156 miles/251 km
Rosslare - 71 miles/114 km

Rail Service:
Dublin - Wicklow Town
Rosslare - Wicklow Town
Airport: None

Tourist Office:
Wicklow Town
Tel: 0404 69117
 Open All Year.

CARLOW
Population: 40,988 (1986)
Land Area: 895 km2

CARLOW TOWN:
Population: 11,509
Distance from:
Dublin - 82 km
Cork - 186 km
Shannon - 165 km
Rosslare - 93 km

Rail Service:
Dublin - Carlow Town
Airport: None

Tourist Office:
Carlow Town
Tel: 0503/31554
June-August

COUNTY WICKLOW/CARLOW

The wild heather covered glens and mountains of County Wicklow are within a half hours drive from Ireland's capital. Wicklow is the garden of Ireland and the playground of Dubliners who come to walk and picnic in its stunning countryside. Its name is an English corruption of the Danish "Wyking Alo" meaning "Viking Meadow". Wicklow's landscape is one of high mountain peaks, heathery glens and lakes, forests and golden beaches. As such it offers many possibilities for a broad range of outdoor activities. The county has a growing population of 100,000, many of whom commute to work in Dublin. The main commuter towns are Bray, Greystones and Blessington. The Victorian resort towns of Bray and Arklow have a wide range of industries including Avoca Woollen Mills and Arklow Pottery. In the more rugged west and central parts of the county, sheep farming is common while the land is more fertile nearer the coast.

Historically the county was part of the kingdom of the Leinster kings but the Vikings did establish towns at Arklow and Wicklow. The countryside is dotted with ancient churches and stately homes. The important early christian site of Glendalough (Valley of Two Lakes) is set amongst spectacular scenery. Founded by St Kevin in AD 520, the monastic remains are among the best in the country.

The beautiful glens and vales of Wicklow have inspired artists and poets for centuries. The Vale of Avoca is immortalised in the romantic poetry of Thomas Moore's "The Meeting of the Waters". One of the most spectacular glens is Glencree which curves from near the base of the Sugarloaf Mountain to the foot of the Glendoo Mountain. Nearby is the magnificent Powerscourt Estate and Gardens. On the estate is a beautiful waterfall, the highest in Ireland (122m).

West Wicklow is relatively less well known than the eastern part and is ruggedly beautiful. Near the town of Blessington is the 18th century paladian mansion, Russborough House. Its art collection is a major attraction and includes paintings by Rubens, Gainsborough and Guardi.

County Carlow is the second smallest county in Ireland. It has a varied landscape, from the Blackstairs Mountains (Mt Leinster 796 m) in the east to the rich rolling farmland in the rest of the county. With two large rivers, the Slaney and the Barrow, winding their way through the county, there are excellent opportunities for fishing and boating. There is also pleasant hill climbing and mountain walking in the Slievemargey Hills and the Blackstairs mountains.
Many of the towns in the county were Anglo-Norman strongholds and the county has many fine surviving monastic sites, abbeys and castles. Well worth a visit are the beautiful ruins of the once great monastic settlement at St Mullins. Carlow Town, the county capital, is a pleasant town on the river barrow and was once an Anglo-Norman stronghold. Near to Carlow Town is the impressive Brownshill Dolmen who's capstone, weighing 101.6 tonnes, is the largest in Europe.

ACCOMMODATION

WHERE TO SHOP

**THE GLENDALOUGH HOTEL
GLENDALOUGH,
CO. WICKLOW**
TeL: 0404/45135
Fax: 0404/45142

The Glendalough Hotel is now offering more facilities and an increased standard of comfort to all our guests. Located in the heart of Ireland's Garden County, the hotel offers the weary traveller comfortable and tastefully decorated bedrooms with a range of special offers. An excellent restaurant, built over the Glendasan river, offers good quality food and fine wines served in a tranquil atmosphere. The new Glendalough Tavern Lounge offers an extensive and reasonably priced bar food menu to meet all your food and drink requirements.

**AVOCA HANDWEAVERS
AVOCA VILLAGE &
KILMACANOGUE
CO WICKLOW**
Tel: 0402-35105 &
01-2867466

Avoca Handweavers boasts Ireland's oldest mill dating back to 1723.
Today in AVOCA VILLAGE the mill still operates from the whitewashed buildings where (on a free tour) you can see the whole handweaving process bring the colours alive in the famous Avoca tweeds and woollens. You can then enjoy a browse in the mill shop & relax in the restaurant. At KILMACANOGUE you will find our 2nd shop and craft centre with gardens & renowned restaurant. Open every day 9.30am – 5.30pm.

DISCOVER NORTHERN IRELAND

An area of outstanding beauty, where you can find some of the best fishing, golfing, cruising in the world and where the quality of arts and entertainment match that of the sporting activities - this is the lesser-known face of Northern Ireland, a region that now attracts more than one million visitors a year. The tourist industry is extremely important to the province, supporting 10,000 employees and generating £153m in visitor revenue.

The province's tourism infrastructure is being radically developed, leading to more hotels with leisure facilities, better quality guesthouse accommodation, more attractions like the Northern Ireland Aquarium at Portaferry, the Butterfly Farm at Seaforde, Peatlands Country Park near Dungannon, modern sea-fishing boats, more fishing stands, caravan sites, viewpoints and picnic sites. Hotels, guesthouses, farm and country houses and self-catering accommodation, which are approved by the NITB, are listed in the publication "Where to Stay". The local food (salmon, trout, seafood, big steaks, the famous Ulster fry, game and a great variety of home baked bread) is excellent. Roscoff, a restaurant in Belfast, has been awarded one of only two Michelin Stars to be given to restaurants in all Ireland.

Northern Ireland is richly endowed with superb golf courses, attracting players from all over the world. Some 70 courses in this small country almost make the province itself one vast course.

The two best-known courses are Royal Co Down at Newcastle and Royal Portrush in Co Antrim, both championship links and there are others of championship standard.

For hire cruising enthusiasts who are tired of not being able to see the water for the boats, there is still one unspoilt, uncluttered and beautiful waterway in the British Isles, Lough Erne in Co Fermanagh. A paradise for birds, wild flowers, fishing and cruising, Lough Erne is a magnificent island-studded 50 mile long waterway.

The Erne Charter Boat Association represents six cruiser companies, which maintain fleets of fully equipped modern cruisers to a high standard and provide excellent shoreside facilities. There is no need to write to individual charter firms; one letter to the Lakeland Visitor Centre, Shore Road, Enniskillen, Co Fermanagh will bring you the

"Holidays Afloat" brochure, which gives an illustration of all the boats with details of their accommodation and equipment.

For the angling fraternity, Co Fermanagh has arguably some of the finest fishing water in Europe. Lough Erne has claimed many world coarse angling match records and one of the top coarse angling competitions in Europe is the "P & O European Ferries Classic Fishing Festival", held on Lough Erne in Co Fermanagh every May, with £15,000 prize money to be won.

The game fishing is excellent too. Lough Melvin has a good run of Spring salmon and grilse and several interesting kinds of trout, including gillaroo, sonaghan (which looks like a fighting sea trout) and an Ice Age predecessor of the trout - the char.

Of course there is excellent fishing in other parts of Northern Ireland. In the Foyle area the principal salmon and sea trout rivers extend to over 200 miles. In addition there is the massive game fish-rich network of rivers flowing into Lough Neagh, the largest freshwater lake in the British Isles.

No part of Northern Ireland is more than an hour's drive from the sea, and the 300 miles of coastline offers some of the best mixed fishing you'll find anywhere.

120

If, however you are interested in catching some beautiful scenery, the 80-mile Antrim Coast Road from Larne to Portrush is one of the most scenic in Britain. The fabled Glens of Antrim, each with its place in Irish folklore, are lovely green valleys running to the sea. From Fair Head you can see Rathlin Island, six miles out, with the hills and islands of Scotland beyond. Rathlin can be reached by boat from Ballycastle, which hosts the historic Oul'Lammas Fair each August. Beyond the famous Carrick-a-Rede Rope Bridge, is the

lovely secluded beach of Whitepark Bay and the smallest church in Ireland at Portbraddan. The World Heritage site of the Giant's Causeway is a fascinating collection of hexagonal basalt columns formed, some say, by volcanic activity, though others prefer the more colourful legend that it was built by the Ulster giant Finn McCool. Nearby is the famous Old Bushmills Distillery, the oldest licensed whiskey distillery in the world.

In the south of the province, you can walk for hours in the dramatic mountains of Mourne which "sweep down to the sea" near Newcastle. This is good horse riding country and if you're interested in history, you can trace the footsteps of the patron saint of Ireland, St Patrick, at Saul, where he built his first church, and at Downpatrick where he is buried. Visit the Georgian mansion at Castleward on the way to the car ferry across Strangford Lough and enjoy the pleasant drive up the Ards Peninsula, through an area of old churches, country houses, villages and beaches.

There's a wealth of places to visit - from Stone Age Standing Stones in the Sperrin mountains, the Ulster Folk and Transport Museum and the Ulster American Folk Park, Norman castles to the Georgian townhouses of Hillsborough and Armagh.

And when in Belfast, the Grand Opera House, Botanic Gardens and Victorian pubs all beckon - along with theatre, restaurants and a wide variety of entertainment.

Photos: Northern Ireland Tourist Board.